Snags and Sawyers:

2000 Miles
Down the Arkansas River

As told by:

John Evert, Dick Henke, & Jerry Pankow

Commentary by Terri Evert Karsten

WAGONBRIDGE PUBLISHING

2012

Snags and Sawyers: 2000 Miles Down the Arkansas River

Editor: Terri Karsten
Assistant editor: Alyssa Koenig
Map design: Kayla Fayerweather

WAGONBRIDGE PUBLISHING

Cover Photo: Mississippi River Sunrise, June 2012

Wagonbridge Publishing
661 East Howard
Winona, MN 55987-4302 U.S.A.
Orders at Wagonbridge Publishing:
        wagonbridgepublishing.com

Copyright © 2012 by Terri Karsten

First Edition Softcover
ISBN 978-0-9828552-1-8

CAN DO
ADVENTURES

For Dad

The paddle on the right is one of the original paddles used by Johnny Evert in 1949. He acquired the paddle on the left later, when he had a sailboat.

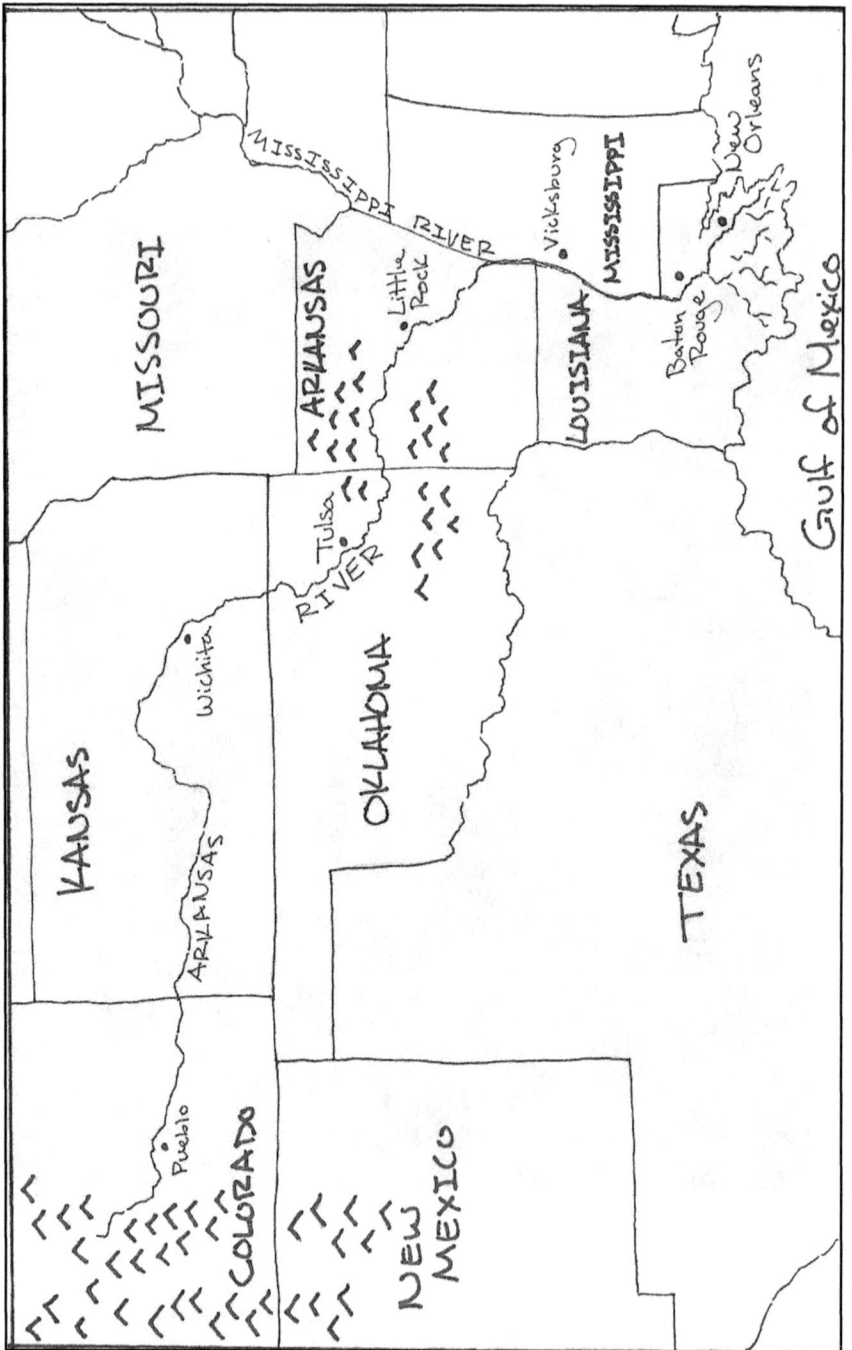

All maps by Kayla Fayerweather

Table of Contents

May, 1949. John Evert, Jerry Pankow, and Dick Henke prepared for their journey by practicing on the Upper Arkansas River.

Introduction

Three restless youths, two cedar canoes, one long river.

The war was over, but it haunted them still. Today we would call it post traumatic stress disorder, but in 1949 no one talked about the trouble veterans had in readjusting to civilian life. Johnny, Dick, and Jerry didn't talk about it either. Instead, they went on a two month, 2000 mile canoe trip on an untamed river.

Johnny Evert, at 22, was the oldest of the three. Born in Kansas, he lived in many places in the Midwest before his family settled in Denver. As a boy, Johnny loved spending summers at the family cabin in Silver Plume, a small mining town in the Rockies. Johnny remembered fishing in the stream with blasting caps and walking two miles down the mountain to the nearest library in Georgetown. Johnny's first job was in a butcher shop when he was 12. In his teens, he worked in the mines near Silver Plume. Before he finished high school, he spent a season as a gandydancer (a railroad worker who lays track) in the Rockies, though he soon became the crew's cook. During Johnny's senior year of high school, the United States was still fighting World War II. Johnny tried to enlist in the various branches of the military, but was turned away so often it became a joke. Once a week he went to the Denver Marine offices. At 6'1", he was very thin - 27" waist, 132 lbs - but he couldn't pass the eye test. He wanted to be a marine, like John Wayne. He even skipped school and tried to enlist in the Navy, but they confirmed he was too blind. Then, on his 18th birthday, as he graduated at the top of his class from Regis High School, he was handed a diploma and a letter from the President: he was drafted. By this time he had memorized the eye chart, so he could get in. After basic training he became a drill instructor, then a sergeant. He learned to drive trucks and tanks, and how to use machine guns, bazookas, and dynamite. As a draftee, Johnny had no set discharge date, so at this point, he enlisted to change his status and was sent to Korea for a tour of duty there. After his discharge, Johnny went to Denver University on the GI bill, where he studied engineering. When he wasn't studying, Johnny went skiing. A hot-shot ski bum, he worked with the ski patrol and taught skiing lessons.

Dick Henke, 21, grew up in Denver, Colorado, graduating from South High. Tall and lean, he excelled in the high hurdles, though he was never able to beat his rival from Denver East High, Jerome Biffle, who went on to win the Olympics. Dick was drafted into military service after high school. He soon made sergeant, enlisted to change his draft status to regular army, and was sent to Korea.

Dick met Johnny in the service when Johnny was assigned as his drill sergeant. The two hit it off immediately. Both were born daredevils, ready to try anything. Dick's brother, Bob, said whenever one started something the other was right there with him. Like Johnny, Dick was crazy about skiing, so much so that he skied on glaciers even when the regular season was over, even when the

8

snow cover gave way to gravel. Once he shattered his knee skiing off a cliff in the mountains. He and Johnny both loved breaking trail in the high Rockies. But Dick's greatest love was flying. He started flying a biplane in the 1940's, and became one of the first pilots to fly radio controlled airplanes. When Dick returned from the war, it was no surprise that he majored in airline management at Denver University.

Jerry Pankow, the youngest of the three, was 20. He attended church with Dick and Dick's brother, Bob, at St. John's Lutheran Church in Denver. Jerry enlisted after his high school graduation. His army days were spent in Germany, with the Fifth Field Artillery, 1st Infantry Division. By 1949, he was also a student on the GI bill at Denver University, studying chemistry.

Like both Dick and Johnny, Jerry was also an avid skier. He worked for the ski patrol in the mountains above Denver and kept busy with Walther League, a young people's group at St. John's. Jerry played the lead in one of the Walther League amateur theater productions. He was also involved with Walther League square dancing and worked 40 hours a week while he was taking classes at Denver University.

They planned an epic journey from Pueblo, Colorado to mouth of the Arkansas River, then onto the Mississippi and south to New Orleans by canoe. As far as they could tell, the first, and possibly the last time anyone had traveled from Colorado to New Orleans by canoe was in the 1880's, when a couple of trappers made the trip in three months, starting about 30 miles below Pueblo. The trio figured their trip would set a new record, both for time and distance on the Arkansas in a craft without power.

In many ways, the timing of this trip was perfect for maximum publicity. In the summer of 1949, the Arkansas River was under a great deal of scrutiny as Governor Kerr of Oklahoma was particularly interested in river navigation. The Arkansas River was notorious for alternately low water and flooding. As early as the 1930's many commercial interests wanted to develop the river to improve navigation. In 1935 the U.S. Army Corps of Engineers determined that although it would be possible to develop the river for navigation, it would be too expensive to be economically feasible. In spite of this report, Congress went ahead with plans to establish flood control on the river. Then World War II interrupted many of the stateside projects, and nothing much was done until 1946. A number of prominent businessmen from Tulsa and the surrounding areas created the Arkansas Basin Development Association (ABDA), and pushed for legislation to improve river navigation. In July of 1946, Congress passed the McClellen-Kerr Arkansas River Navigation system for developing hydropower, navigation, flood control, and recreation in the Arkansas River Basin.

However, the problem of 100 million tons of silt washing down the river continued to delay construction until the 1950's. All this points to the fact that in 1949, the Arkansas River had a very different character than that of the Arkansas River today. With ongoing problems of erratic floods, low water, and silt, the Arkansas River was full of snags and whirlpools, uncertain depth, and unmapped bends. In fact, no one seemed to know exactly how long the river actually was, with newspapers of the time reporting the journey from Pueblo to New Orleans anywhere between 2000 and 2,700 miles. In the 1950's, after this trip, numerous dams were built and the river 'straightened' to some extent, though it still curls and winds its way across Colorado, Kansas, Oklahoma, and Arkansas before reaching the Mississippi; its current length is recorded at 1,460 miles from its headwaters in the Colorado Rockies to its mouth at Napoleon, Arkansas. From that point to New Orleans along the Mississippi River is another some 350 miles by road, but the Mississippi River bends and twists even more than the Arkansas River does, and it changes course periodically from floods and high water, so the actual distance on the river was much more. Variations in depth also make it hard to estimate the course of the river. In fact, the main

10

reason Johnny, Dick and Jerry were able to make this trip at all was because the water in the Arkansas River was particularly high in the summer of 1949, and the Mississippi River also had waters above flood stage.

Johnny, Dick, and Jerry weren't worried by the wild state of the Arkansas River. With aerial maps as their primary guides, and more enthusiasm than experience in a canoe, they thought paddling just such a river would be the perfect challenge. Taking off on a trek some 2,000 or 3,000 miles across six states takes a special kind of courage, or as Johnny said, "a certain kind of crazy." At the very least, such a journey requires a spirit of adventure not often found in any age.

More than anything else, the three veterans were restless. They had been to war and come home safe but shaken. Dick and Johnny had faced the bitter cold of Korea. Johnny's nightmares focused on the tractors making the rounds each morning to scoop up the frozen bodies of men, women, and children who had died overnight. On the rare occasions he talked about the war, Johnny revealed his fear of walking to the latrine at night with his gun cocked and ready. When the three young men returned, it was hard to settle in to ordinary life in the States. After leading a company of men, Sergeant John Evert found sitting in a college classroom increasingly difficult. Even though the freshmen were only three or four years younger than he was, they seemed so naive. "They were children, really," he said. So the friends, Johnny, Dick, and Jerry grumbled over their beers and dreamed of something grander. Then they went beyond the dream.

"Some guys spend their whole lives dreaming," Johnny said. "We decided to do something."

This is their story, gleaned from the letters Dick and Johnny sent home, newspapers and radio programs chronicling the trip, photographs and 8 mm movies, and a diary they wrote along the way. Smudged and faded over the years, the diary was written in pencil in a small, black, ringed notebook, a little more than 3 1/2" by 5". All three men added to the diary, often while sitting beside a campfire on a remote sandbar. In the six decades since the journal was written, several pages from the beginning of the diary have been lost. Exposure to wet conditions has made some words throughout the diary illegible. In spite of these difficulties, the diary provides an interesting, ongoing perspective of the trip as it unfolded. Numerous conversations with John Evert have clarified difficult passages and added additional details. In order to allow the reader to distinguish between the letters, the diary and editorial notes from other sources including these conversations, I have used the following conventions:

Letters appear in this font with [ ] for parts that are illegible. I have edited letters for spelling and some grammar.

Diary entries appear in this font with [ ] indicating parts that are illegible. Diary entries have been edited for spelling and grammar only when necessary for understanding.

All other portions of the text are in this font, indicating editorial notes based on research, newspaper articles, radio programs, and conversations with John Evert, Jerry Pankow, and Bob Henke (Dick's brother.).

The three men kept a diary of the trip. Unfortunately, the first several pages of the diary have been lost. The trip started on June 12, 1949, but the first remaining entry is July 1, 1949.

Jerry, Johnny, and Dick planned the trip using aerial survey maps.

Prologue

December 1948 to June 11, 1949
Denver, Colorado

The idea of the river trip germinated in a Denver bar one December evening in 1948. Conversation rolled around to summer and the end of the ski season. Since they couldn't ski in the summer, Johnny insisted they would need something else to keep them busy. Why not take a trip? Why not go to New Orleans? In fact, why not paddle all the way there on the Arkansas River? Just because no one else had done it didn't mean they couldn't. But when they told family and friends they wanted to canoe down the Arkansas, everyone said it was impossible. Of course, that made these three young men all the more determined to try.

In spite of this determination, Johnny, Dick, and Jerry knew making the trip a reality would be extremely difficult. The first obstacle was money. By selling Johnny's car and Dick's motorcycle, then adding Jerry's army savings, they came up with a starting budget of $600. They expected to add to their finances with articles, pictures, and movies taken along the way. They planned to sell everything in New Orleans, and then get a sponsorship from either a radio station or a film company so they could buy motorcycles and drive nonstop for a record breaking trip home.

In the spring of 1949, they began gathering the gear they would need for a two to three month journey, most of it outdoors, camping rough. They packed a tent, sleeping bags, a gas stove, insect bombs, a radio, Mae West Life preservers, mess kits, canteens, clothes, a movie camera, three still shot cameras, two .22 calibre rifles, a pistol, and fishing equipment; about 300 pounds of equipment in all. They carried enough food for three days and enough water for two, hoping to supplement the canned goods they brought with fresh fish. Maybe they would even have a bit of luck hunting, since all three were good shots. Hunting and fishing would help add variety to their diet, especially since they had only $100 each for buying additional food along the way. Of course, hunting and fishing regulations were different in 1949 than they are today. Each state managed its own regulations as they still do, but those regulations were much lest strict and not as widely enforced.

Less practical than food, but equally important, Johnny, Dick, and Jerry carried a letter of introduction from Colorado's governor, William Lee Knous, to Louisiana's governor, Earl K. Long. The two governors were friends, and the young men expected the letter would increase publicity for the trip.

The next step was choosing the right watercraft. Dick ordered two 10 1/2 foot kayak kits from Sears and put them together. They were open pit kayaks however, which did not work well in rough water. In the weeks before the trip,

Jerry and Johnny hold up the larger canoe. At 117 pounds, it was fairly awkward to handle on land.

Johnny, Dick, and Jerry shot the rapids on the Arkansas River above Pueblo and decided the kayaks were not seaworthy. The crafts sat too low in the water and couldn't handle the churning rapids. Snags and rocks tore holes in the canvas even when the young men practiced on the much milder Platte River. They ended up getting an 18 foot cedar and canvas canoe weighing 117 lbs, and a second cedar canoe. The second canoe, 17 feet long and weighing 124 lbs, was smaller than the first, but heavier and hard to handle alone. They planned to rotate every two hours or so because paddling alone was hard, though Johnny later admitted he actually preferred the smaller, single man canoe because he liked being alone.

It would be easy to believe at this point the young men were ready for anything, so their lack of any extensive boating experience comes as a surprise. They had all been in a canoe before for purely recreational paddling, but never on an extended trip. To remedy this obstacle, the three of them spent weekends before the trip practicing on area rivers like the Platte River near Denver. Practice was rough. In a pre-trip article in the Denver Post, Dick reported, "Last time we were out on the river, we ran the canoe through three barbed wire fences and over two dams. We were swamped twice and filled our camping stove full of water. But we're learning fast." (*Denver Post*, June, 1949)

Dick, Johnny and Berniece Fischer are ready to transport the canoe to the river.

Johnny talks to the radio announcer in Pueblo. Behnd him on the left, Berniece Fischer, Johnny's future wife, looks on. Johnny, Dick, and Jerry relied on radio and newspapers to publicize their adventure.

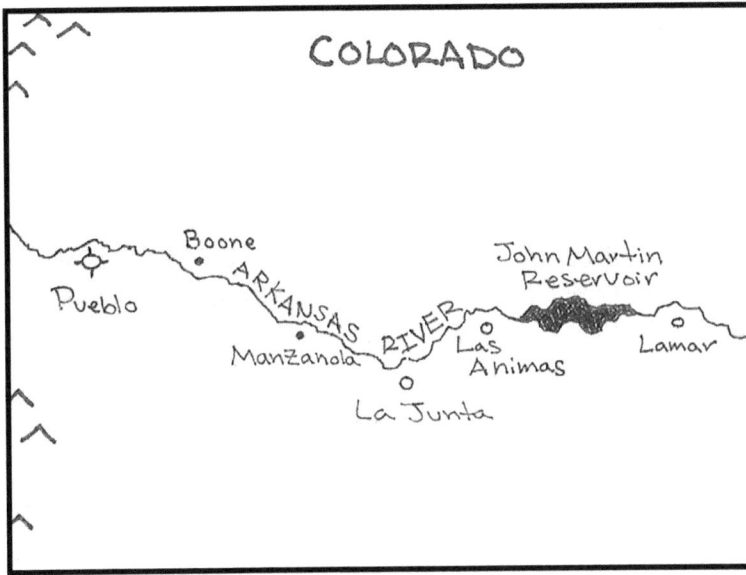

How much water?

June 12 to June 18
Pueblo, Colorado to John Martin Reservoir, Colorado

Pueblo, Colorado (Pop. 63, 685)[1]

Pueblo, Colorado's strategic position at the confluence of the Arkansas River and Fountain Creek has made it ideal for settlement even before Europeans explored the area in the 17th and 18th centuries. The current city of Pueblo began as a small fort at the river junction in 1842. At that time the Arkansas River formed part of the border between the United States and Mexico. Pueblo was a major city in Colorado both socially and economically until a devastating series of floods up to 1921 destroyed one third of the downtown businesses. Prone to both drought and flood, the city sits on the 'high desert' of the Colorado plains, at the edge of the Rocky

---

[1]   All population figures are taken from the 1950 US census unless otherwise noted.

Mountains. Though the area does not usually get much rain, the day scheduled for departure promised to be wet.

Sunday, June 12

Heavy, water-logged clouds darkened the afternoon sky on the day of the launch, but the gloom did not dampen the spirits of the crowd gathered to watch Dick, Jerry, and Johnny take off. Nearly one hundred people milled about on the soggy bank of the Arkansas River, near the interstate bridge, a cantilevered, steel bridge with arches. The river, swollen from recent rains, churned a muddy brown. Reporters from Pueblo's KGHF radio station and the Denver Post newspaper interviewed the young men beside the river. In pictures of this last pre-launch interview, standing off to the side

The crowd gathers on the day of the launch. Nearly 100 people came to see them off. Johnny pushed the big canoe off first, with Jerry in the front, and Dick steering from the rear.

and smiling widely is a young woman, Berniece Fischer. Pretty and fresh in a print dress, she and Johnny had started dating not long before. Johnny isn't looking at her in the pictures, intent instead on the radio announcer. But the further downstream he went, the more she took up residence in his thoughts, until he dreamed only of coming back to marry her. Still, at that moment, the coming adventure took the forefront.

At 3:00 p.m. a sudden downpour drenched the onlookers. As the crowd scattered, the young men pushed off from shore and swirled out of sight. Rain pelted the river, almost capsizing their canoes.

Twenty minutes later, five miles east of Pueblo at the next bridge, they beached the canoes and set up camp on a sandbar, in what would be the first of many such wet camps over the next two months. The young men's worried parents drove out from Pueblo to meet them at the bridge, just to make sure they were all okay. After reassuring the folks everything was fine, the canoeists fixed a meal and bedded down, planning for an early start the next day, when they would sweep past Boone, Colorado and under the Nepesta Bridge.

Nepesta Bridge
Boone, Colorado

Nepesta Bridge spans the Arkansas River near Boone, Colorado, about 30 miles southeast of Pueblo. Views from the east and the south are shown here. Built in 1905, this bridge was the only roadway truss bridge to survive the 1921 Arkansas River flood. (Photos by Steve Eller, Historic American Engineering Record, Library of Congress)

The Manzanola Bridge shown here was built in 1908, was replaced in 1950, one year after the canoeists shot underneath. (Photo by Clayton Fraser, U.S. Dept. of Interior, NPS, U.S. Library of Congress.)

Monday, June 13

The men ran into the roughest waters early in the trip, where debris clogged the Arkansas River. A very fast and tricky current, along with dangerous eddies, whirlpools, and boils made it even more treacherous. Among the first obstacles they had to navigate were the bridges which could have unpredictable currents or hidden log jams beneath the surface.

The paddlers also battled headwinds in this section of the river. The winds slowed them considerably, and pushed the smaller canoe sideways. On Monday, as they were approaching Manzanola, Colorado, Dick lost control of the single man canoe which carried all of their gear. The craft capsized, drenching everything. Fortunately, the waterproof oilcloth-wrapped bundles containing their food, tent, sleeping bags and clothes floated, helping in the recovery, Johnny said later "waterproof" is a fairly inaccurate term.

After this dunking the young men stopped at a sandbar just west of Manzanola to set up camp and let the gear dry overnight. With a wet tent, wet sleeping bags, and no radio, it would have been a miserable night, but no one thought of turning back. A few days after the incident, Dick posted a letter home to his folks. [2]

---

[2]　　The canoeists maintained contact with family and friends by telephone occasionally, though that was expensive, and by mail. They posted letters from any town, and received letters by general delivery. The folks back home sent letters to the post office in the next town. The travelers picked up the mail when they arrived. Any new letters reaching that post office after they left would be forwarded to the next town along the route.

Dear Mom & Dad,

There is no doubt about it, this is one heck of a rugged trip. We have to fight for every inch of ground we cover. I sank the lone boat first day after Pueblo and lost my sunglasses, besides my radio won't work anymore. (it's wet.) Rifle also rusted shut, movie camera got wet and doesn't work too well any more. Sleeping bag has been wet for 2 days, but we're having a wonderful time.

Love, Dick

Manzanola, Colorado (Pop. 543)

This small town has not changed much since 1949. The 2003 census lists the population at 506. By 1876, tracks from the Santa Fe railroad ran through Manzanola, but the depot was not built there until 1913. The Arkansas River flows past the town about a mile north.

Tuesday, June 14

With their gear still wet, the soggy paddlers went past Manzanola without stopping. That night they camped on a sandbar and tried to dry things out, though the soggy weather continued.

La Junta, Colorado (Pop. 7712)

La Junta, which means 'junction' in Spanish, has been a hub of the railroad in the Arkansas River valley since 1875. At first it was an 'end of the line' camp for the railroad workers and consisted of only tents and rough clapboard shanties. When the railroad moved on, the Santa Fe Railroad managers recognized the importance of the location, and built a depot which became the Santa Fe Railroad headquarters in Colorado. A few years later, in 1881, the city incorporated with 285 inhabitants. By the time Jerry, Dick, and Johnny arrived, farming, especially sugar beets, had helped to expand the La Junta's economy.

Swink Bridge: view from northeast to the southwest. This bridge spanned the Arkansas River 15 miles by road southeast of Manzanola. The bridge was built in 1921 and replaced in 1986. (Photo by Historic American Engineering Record, Library of Congress)

Wednesday, June 15

They woke up on Wednesday morning to find the river rising from heavy rains upstream. Water lapped at their sleeping bags. Three soggy days and three wet nights. Combined with the rough weather that made paddling hard work, Johnny, Dick, and Jerry were happy to take a break. They reached the town around noon on Wednesday, docked about two miles below the town's eastern bridge, and took time to meet with the local newspaper reporter, stroll through La Junta's downtown area, and visit the post office. Johnny's thoughts turned to the people back home, most especially Berniece, the girl he left behind. He wrote:

Dearest,
I love you, I love you, I love you! Too tired to write, got here Wed. noon. Please write General Delivery Dodge City, Kansas. I love you. How are things in Denver? I love you. I want only to be with you.
See you in Sept.

Love, love - Johnny

24

John Martin Dam caused more trouble than they expected. (Photo circa 1979, U.S. Army Corps of Engineers.)

Las Animas, Colorado (Pop. 3223)

Las Animas was about half the size of La Junta. The county seat, Las Animas was (and still is) the only incorporated city in the sparsely populated Bent County. In an odd gesture of generosity, the sign welcoming visitors to town these days suggests they visit the nearby historic site of Boggsville, the last home of the famous Kit Carson. Boggsville became a ghost town after the railroad chose to go through Las Animas instead. The canoeists did not stop in Las Animas.

Thursday, June 16 - Friday, June 17

Leaving La Junta, they traveled northeast through Las Animas and toward John Martin Reservoir. The Purgatory River joins the Arkansas River two miles west of Las Animas. In this stretch the water continued rough and the wind hard, but at least the rain stopped. Some of the gear started drying out. Though it was still chilly enough for jackets, the young men took off their shoes and enjoyed the sunshine.

John Martin Reservoir/ Caddoa Lake

This fifteen mile long, six mile wide man-made lake was formed by the John Martin Dam, built in 1948 for water storage and flood control. The resulting lake is now called the John Martin

Reservoir, but in 1949 the new body of water was alternately called John Martin Lake or Caddoa Lake. The land around here is flat, the landscape of the western plains. There are few trees and no mountains. When the dam was built, it was obvious that the resulting lake would inundate the town of Caddoa, which sat in the center of the valley. So, for the second time in its history, the small town moved when construction on the dam began in 1946. The first move had been a few miles upstream in 1879. Today, Caddoa, situated between La Junta and Lamar, boasts three residents.

Saturday, June 18

On the morning of June 18, the canoes entered the blue water of Caddoa Lake. After days of battling through rough water and snags, the open water of the lake invited speed. To take advantage of the stiff wind, and reduce the problem of the smaller canoe spinning, the young men lashed the two canoes together and put up a makeshift sail. They made good time racing before the wind. Then the wind worsened. Waves as high as five feet washed over the gunwales, soaking the still damp gear, and threatening to capsize the crafts. They had to paddle frantically and were lucky to reach the shore. Dick wrote:

Dear Uncle Bill, Aunt Ena, & Allen,
The shmoo is OK. The trip is VERRY RUGGED but so far we have met with no serious mishap. The waves get 4 & 5 ft high in the wind and we've sunk one boat and had to swim for it. The boat floated OK though. We are all sunburned around the hands & feet.
TELL MOM TO WRITE
GARDEN CITY KAN
We expect to be there Sun.
Love, Dick

Sunburned and tired, they continued along the shore of the lake until they came to the dam on the east side and began their portage around it. They had been paddling barefoot, but Jerry's feet got so badly sunburned he could barely walk. He had to put boots on for the portage, but that further damaged his feet, rubbing the huge, inch high blisters raw. With Jerry limping, and Dick and Johnny carrying the canoes, they rounded the dam and looked to the river below.

It was nearly empty. In dismay, they studied the muddy swamp the river had become. Clearly there was not enough water to float a canoe.

The Arkansas River bends and winds through the flat plains of western Colorado and Kansas.

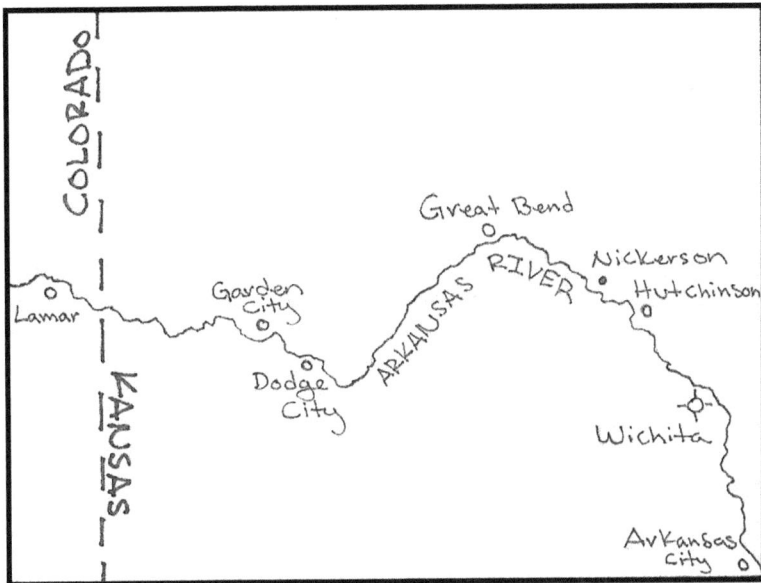

Long Days and Warm Welcomes

June 19 to July 1
Lamar, Colorado to Arkansas City, Kansas

Lamar, Colorado (Pop. 6,820)

Long important as a grazing and timber stop on the Santa Fe Trail, the town of Lamar was established south of the Arkansas River around 1870, when the railroad moved a depot from Blackwell, three miles east of the current site. Mr. Black, the depot owner, objected to donating land to the railroad. The depot was 'stolen' and moved while he was gone to Pueblo. Land speculators renamed the depot to honor the Secretary of the Interior, L. Q. Lamar, so that he would grant them a land office. Lamar is not far from the Amache Internment Camp which was established in 1942 for the forced re-location of Japanese-Americans. The sixteen square mile camp had closed in 1945, less than four years before Johnny, Jerry and Dick

29

came through the area. By 1949, the buildings had been removed, and the rest of the camp had reverted to farmland.

Sunday, June 19

When the river ran out of water, Jerry got a ride ahead with a local farmer while the other two slogged through the mud pushing the canoes. Jerry set up camp in a city park on the riverbank. He lanced his huge blisters with a pocket knife, and then tried drying out the gear while he waited for Johnny and Dick.

After six hours, Dick and Johnny gave up the fight against the mud. With the help of a local farmer, they shipped the canoes to Lamar, about twenty miles east. In Lamar, they found out there had been so much flooding below the dam that the flood gates were closed to prevent further damage downstream. They spent the day in Lamar, trying to figure out what to do. Both Dick and Johnny wrote home about their decision to go on:

Dear Mom & Dad,

We got to John Martin Dam and found that due to flood damage we could not go any further. So shipped boats & stuff to Lamar. We are now sending boats on to Dodge City, Kansas (Write Airmail there). And we are hitch-hiking there. We'll get there one way or the other.

Love, Dick

June 20
Lamar Colorado
Dearest,

Every day I am away I miss you more than I could have possibly imagined. You must know that I love you and soon we will be together for always. Sorry about using a post card, but all letters and everything got wet. No water in the river, but we are going on.

With all my love, Johnny
Please write to Dodge City

30

Garden City, Kansas (Pop. 10,905)

Garden City was the biggest city they had seen since starting over a week earlier. When the town was started in 1878 by the Fulton brothers, there were only four buildings the first year. The rich bottom land of the Arkansas River Valley drew settlers. By July, 1879, there were forty buildings and new settlers filling the town. Despite this promising beginning, rainfall in the area was, and still is, erratic and droughts are common. A fourteen-month drought convinced local investors that irrigation from the Arkansas River was necessary for the town to prosper. The Garden City Ditch, the first major irrigation scheme in Kansas was completed in 1880, leading the way for irrigation throughout the county. Garden City still faced problems as cattlemen in the area tried to discourage the farmers, and the risk of Indian attack was always present. In these challenges, Garden City exemplifies the real "wild west." Wyatt Earp's older half-brother, Newton, served as the first marshall. Still, by 1949, Garden City had become a very welcoming and peaceful town. In fact, the people in Garden City put the canoeists in touch with contacts in Arkansas City. Garden City was also much safer than it had been in those early days, with a regular police force which Johnny, Dick, and Jerry had occasion to meet.

Monday, June 20

After sending the canoes and gear on ahead, the young men spent Monday hitchhiking, following the plan Dick shared with his parents. They got as far as Garden City, Kansas. It was an era when hitch-hiking was an accepted and common form of travel, especially for returning servicemen, but it wasn't always easy to get a ride. It took them almost all day to travel the 102 miles by road. Since their gear had gone ahead of them to Dodge City, they couldn't set up camp. After arriving in town and eating a hot meal at the home of Jerry's dad's friend, Wayne Foster, they all felt better. The night was warm and clear, so they saw no problem sleeping on a park bench.

The local police saw it differently, thinking the young men were vagrants. So to avoid arrest, the travelers booked a room at

The Windsor Hotel in Garden City was much more comfortable than their usual sleeping arrangements. The room would have cost between $2.50 and $3.50. (Photo by Billy Hathorn, 2010.)

the Windsor Hotel in Garden City. Surely a night in a real bed after sleeping rough for nine days felt good, but the unexpected cost dug into their dwindling stores of cash. Johnny's letter, posted the next morning, gives more detail about the three days it took to get from the Reservoir on Saturday to Garden City on Monday.

June 21, 1949
Garden City Kansas
(The Windsor Hotel)

Dearest Berniece,

By now you must know I love only you; my every conscious thought is of you, my love for you and the wonderful times we had together. I only hope that soon we can be together again and that you feel a little of the burning love I hold deep in my heart for you. My dear, every moment I am away from you is pure agony but someday I know in my heart we will be together once again.

Dick and I have had to do all the work since Jerry got his feet sunburned and it has really been bad. We came across Caddoa Lake (John Martin Dam) with the two canoes lashed

32

Dick and Johnny enjoyed swimming, but kept an watchful eye for planes buzzing them. The trio spent most nights camping rough along the river. Note the sleeping bags hanging on the tent to dry.

together and put up a sail. We got going so fast we had to take down the sail and head for shore for the boats were filling with water. Then Dick and I had to carry the boats across the dam and down the other side.
NO water! . . .

One of the men at the Dam gave Jerry a ride into Lamar with all the equipment and Dick and I started pushing the canoes across the dry river. It took us 6 hours to go 2 1/2 miles and then we had to quit. We walked about 5 miles to get a farmer to haul the boats into Lamar and there we shipped the boats and equipment to Dodge City. Then we started hitch-hiking to there. We got as far as Garden City by nightfall and after a lot of trouble we contacted Mr. Pankow's [Jerry's dad] friend who bought us a chicken dinner and some beer. After trying to sleep in the local park, we finally had to get a hotel room since the cops wanted to take us in. Well that's about all the news so with the hope that I will soon get some mail from you, I will close. Please write,
        All my love, Johnny

Tuesday, June 21

Still hitchhiking, they left Garden City early in the morning and reached Dodge City, 46 miles by road, later that day. That afternoon, the young men had lunch with Johnny's cousins, Sharon and Mary Margaret Evert, and his Aunt Alice. His uncle Frank was the manager of the creamery in Dodge City. Although he had not seen them for many years, the family was delighted to entertain Johnny and his friends and hear the story of their river trip.

Dodge City (Pop. 11,262)

Francisco Vasquez de Coronado crossed the Arkansas River near where Dodge City was later established. Built on the busy Santa Fe Trail, Dodge City became infamous as the toughest town on the frontier. In 1872, eleven years before Garden City was incorporated, George M. Hoover set up a bar in a tent since alcohol was prohibited at Fort Dodge, five miles to the east. By August, the town was organized as 'Buffalo City', but the name had to be changed to avoid confusion with Buffalo, Kansas. Dodge City was not incorporated until 1875, and at first there was no formal law enforcement. Some fifteen people were killed in 1872 alone. Concerned businessmen tried hiring a private lawman. When that didn't work, they established a vigilante committee, which soon proved to be as violent as the outlaws. For years the conflict continued between the people wanting an 'open' town with gambling, drinking and 'loose' women and people wanting a town ruled by law and order.

However, Dodge City's notoriety was of far less interest to the three men than the depth of the water in the Arkansas River. At this point it was finally deep enough to resume paddling.

Wednesday, June 22

Back on the river at last, Johnny, Dick, and Jerry continued on their way, making camp that night on a sandbar down river. Here the river travels through Ford County, crosses a corner of Kiowa County, and then cuts diagonally across Edwards county. This stretch of the river is quite shallow. Today, it's possible to wade across in many places. In 1949, the water depth was unpredictable and varied widely depending on rains to the west. For most of the trip, the water was higher than usual and above flood stage in many areas. In fact, the main reason the water was so low in the stretch after the reservoir was because so much of the river was flooded, and officials had closed the flood gates. This unpredictable, alternating low and high water is part of what has always made the Arkansas River so difficult to navigate.

Thursday, June 23

As they continued east, the young men noticed that the character of the river had changed again, with a slightly slower current and deeper water. The broad plains of Kansas stretched outward from the river, and the sun grew even more intense. In spite of river debris and snags, they navigated this section of the river without further mishap.

Great Bend, Kansas (Pop. 12,665)

East of Dodge City, the Arkansas River meanders southeast for some 20 or 25 miles, then curves gently until it is flowing more north/northeast. At Great Bend, the river turns again to flow southeast once more. The town of Great Bend is named for this sweeping turn at the northern most point of the Arkansas River in Kansas. Like many of the towns established on the Kansas plains in the last half of the 19th century, Great Bend started as a camp for buffalo hunters. The Great Bend Town Company began the town in 1871 because they knew the railroad was coming. After the railroad arrived in 1873, Great Bend became well known as a cattle shipping point, and for a few years was another wild Kansas cowtown. In the 1930's the discovery of oil and gas brought new jobs to the area, and the population nearly doubled in that decade.

Friday, June 24

Johnny, Dick, and Jerry picked up mail in Great Bend, Kansas and sent their own letters to the folks back home. Johnny wrote:

June 24, Great Bend KS
Dearest Berniece,

Got your swell letter after long impatient
waiting. It was nice but please write more often
if you can. Will write a long letter in Wichita but
don't have the time here. Just a short stop.
Kansas is hot and I am hotter if that is possible.
I have gained about 4 pounds and eating like a
horse. Well honey, so long for now but remember
that I love you.

Johnny

The hard work of paddling, fighting wind and currents, made all the
young men hungry most of the time. Dick also wrote home about
his huge appetite.

Dear Mom & Pop

I'll try to call you from Wichita, Kan. in
3 or 4 days. The river is higher now but so
cluttered up with fallen trees that at times it's
quite dangerous. I've picked up quite an appetite.
We ate dinner in town tonight and I had 3
hamburgers, pie alamode, 2 candy bars and a
glass of milk. I've gained 5 lbs. and am in
good health although tired. (Write me in Tulsa Okla.)

Love
Dick

Saturday, June 25

By now the young men were used to paddling all day, and
camping on the riverbanks at night, but food and water was a constant concern. Johnny, Dick, and Jerry really appreciated the com-
plementary homemade dinners from friendly townsfolk along the
way and jars of soup gifted by motherly women. But mostly their
food was monotonous. For breakfast they usually fried up a batch of

pancakes, eating as many as eight or nine each. Lunch consisted of plain bread with apple butter. Suppers in camp had a bit more variety, alternating between sauerkraut and potatoes, beans and chili, and canned spaghetti, often with a mug of steamy hot chocolate to close out the day. They brought along a few army style prepared meals, but abandoned them as tasteless. The one time John tried cooking such a prepared meal, he added water at the wrong time and it became an awful green paste. Overall, they ate a lot of canned beans.

Finding adequate drinking water posed another problem. The river water was too muddy and unsafe for drinking. They needed over a quart a day each and had to replenish the big jugs every other day or so when they stopped in a town. As they went further downstream, they also took salt tablets as a way to avoid heat stroke. Although both Johnny and Dick claimed they gained weight, in reality all three lost weight by the time they came home, in spite of eating a lot whenever they could.

Nickerson, Kansas (Pop. 1,013)

In 1872, the Atchison, Topeka and Santa Fe railroad built a depot near the current location of Nickerson, but no one lived there until after a schoolhouse was built in 1875. In 1878, a new town site was laid out and within 60 days nearly 20 new buildings had been erected. Located 12 miles northwest of Hutchinson, Nickerson is the second largest city in Reno County, Kansas.

Sunday, June 26

As they continued downstream, news of the adventurers preceded them, and curious onlookers waited and watched for their arrival. Sometimes fishermen or kids playing by the river saw them pass and sent word on ahead. Other times, the reporters and followers on the bridges waved as the canoes swept underneath. At 2 p.m. Sunday afternoon, they were spotted as they passed under the Nickerson Bridge. The bridges in Kansas often caused the trio problems with narrow spans and tricky currents making it hard to get through, but they had no trouble with the Nickerson Bridge and raised their paddles in salute to the crowd watching from the bridge deck.

Hutchinson, Kansas (Pop. 33,515)

Like many other towns built in the 1870's in the Arkansas River Valley, Hutchinson was founded because of the railroad. In 1871, Hutchinson was established where the railroad crossed the river. In 1887, a thick vein of rock salt was discovered in Hutchinson. Soon Hutchinson had the first salt processing plant west of the Mississippi River. Now in 2012, the salt mine, 650 feet underground, houses a museum and a secure underground storage facility ideal for film and paper.

When Johnny, Dick, and Jerry went through Hutchinson, memories of World War II were still fresh. Hutchinson had been the site of a small POW camp, housing almost a hundred German and Italian prisoners of war.

FLOATING DOWN ETC.—Three Denver university students were floating and paddling down the Arkansas river Monday, due to dock at Wichita Tuesday night, on their way to New Orleans. They are John Evert, Jerry Pankow and Dick Henke, shown in their two canoes, one of which carries their camping gear.

John Evert, Dick Henke and a reporter discuss the travelers' plans. Photo and caption from Dick Henke's scrapbook, originally published in the Hutchinson News-Herald, June 28, 1949.

Monday, June 27

High winds buffeted the canoes on the way into Hutchinson, delaying them and making the 12 mile trip from Nickerson take four hours. They arrived in Hutchinson at 6 p.m. and tied up in Carey Park, by the beautiful stone boathouse, where the reporter from the Hutchinson-News Herald was waiting to interview them. Hot and tired, they were looking forward to cold ice cream. J. O Tennant, who had always wanted to canoe the Arkansas River, invited them into his home for dinner and a much needed bath.

Johnny sent Berniece a picture post card from Hutchinson, showing blue water lapping against the stone wharf and wooden dock at Carey Park.

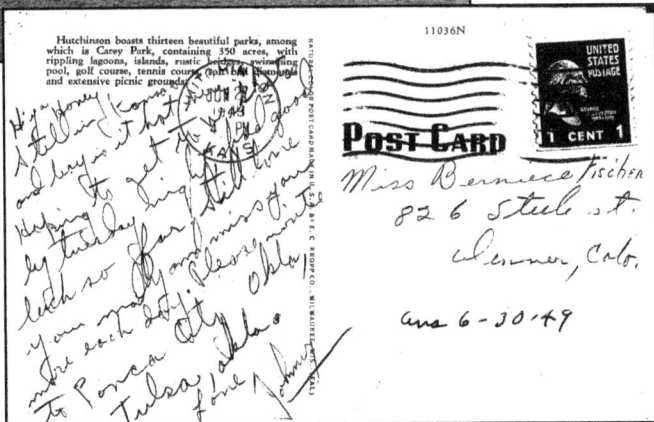

June 27, Hutchinson KS
Hi Honey,

Still in Kansas and boy is it hot here. Hoping to get to Wichita by Tuesday night. Had good luck so far still love you madly and miss you more each day. Please write to Ponca City, Okla, [or] Tulsa Okla.
Love, Johnny.

Tuesday, June 28

In 1923 the entire area between Hutchinson and Wichita had major flooding in June. In 1949, the river was wide and shallow, making a slow current. That, along with high winds and heat, meant they were not able to travel as quickly as they had planned.

Wichita, Kansas (Pop. 168, 279)

Wichita sits at the junction of the Arkansas River and the Little Arkansas River, an ideal meeting place which shows evidence of human habitation for thousands of years. In 1863, a group of Wichita Indians settled there to avoid conflict with pro-Southern tribes during the Civil War. After the war, the Indians were 'removed' but the trading post established there flourished, and Wichita became a base on the Chisholm Trail. Incorporated in 1870, Wichita continued to grow with the arrival of the railroad in 1872. Cattle driven from Texas were shipped east from Wichita, until the 1880's when barbed wire blocked the Chisholm Trail, and Texan cattle drives shifted to Dodge City. Wichita became more important for shipping grain. In the early part of the 20th century, oil was discovered, bringing new industry and growth. Then during the two world wars, Wichita became a center of the airline industry, producing a quarter of all commercial aircraft in the United States by 1929. Newspapers from 1949 reveal Wichita was a scheduled stop on the first commercial Transcontinental and Western Air cross-country flight originating in San Francisco, and terminating in New York with several stops in between. Although Johnny, Dick, and Jerry were using far more primitive transportation, they were following a long tradition of stopping in Wichita in their travels through southeastern Kansas.

Top: The stop in Wichita gave the travelers time for much-needed repairs. From left: Johnny, Jerry, and Dick. (Photo by permission of *AP Wire Photo*. June, 1949.)

Below: In Wichita they set up camp on a sandbank behind the Broadview Hotel. From left: Jerry, Johnny, and Dick. (Photo by permission of *Wichita Eagle*, June, 1949.)

Wednesday, June 29

From the beginning, Jerry, Dick, and Johnny planned several stops along the way, especially in Kansas where they had some family friends and relatives. Wichita was one such prearranged stop. Here they washed their clothes, stocked up on food, and patched the canoes. Rough water and lots of snags had done a fair amount of damage, so both canoes really needed attention. The young men hoped the river would have better conditions after Wichita.

The stop in Wichita also gave them a chance to catch up on mail. Johnny wrote Berniece, answering the questions she asked in her letter to him.

June 29 (written middle of night, posted on June 30)
Wichita, KS (from the Eaton Hotel)
Dearest Berniece,

Sorry to have to use pencil but it is better than nothing. Now to answer your questions one at a time. Traveling is a lot better now but we work harder to make good mileage. The current is pretty slow and the river is wide but shallow. We have had high winds for the past two days and that makes it bad.

Jerry got 1st degree sunburns plus water exposure burns on his feet but fortunately he is better now. Now both Dick and Jerry have had burns (sun) on their hands. Mosquitoes don't bother us too much but flies do. We carry mosquito repellant and that takes care of them but the flies actually like the stuff. Chiggers too. Couldn't sleep very much in the hotel room, too darn soft. Not used to civilization I guess. Movie camera stayed dry but most of our other stuff is wet. We spent a day here in Wichita drying out and resting. Lots of good pictures I hope. Have had lots of fun so far and met some swell people but it is really hard work.

As you probably noticed, I spelled Wichita wrong but I didn't know the difference. As to whether or not I meant what I said in those other and this letters, you

42

should know by now that I do. If you are still in doubt, you have only my word-my life and heart. I know that you can't possibly feel the same as I do since I don't think it possible that you or anyone else could love a person as much as I love you. This isn't just idle or wishful thought, I really mean it and have meant it all along. I don't know how I can convince you but at least I can try. If I get hurt, it won't be your fault. I made the mistake of going with a nice girl, one that I wanted to marry. It would have been better if I had fallen for some Curtis street witch[1] that I could marry at the drop of a hat and been miserable the rest of my life but you came along and I fell like a ton of bricks. Anyway, I meant what I said, and I'll try not to brood -impossible- but I'll try.

I got a letter from you dated June 27, please disregard all references to writing. I was in a very bad mood, the weather was hot, I was hot, mad, thirsty, tired, hungry and in general P.O.d (Not at you.) As to your being confused as to where we are, I am too. Would like to hear more about what you do and about that ski jump at Estes Park. Please keep dreaming about me-I know that sounds kind of funny but I believe that if you think enough about me you might get to like me a little. I look forward to your letters constantly but I know that it isn't your fault. Anyway, you know that I always think of you and love you. I am awfully tired and have to get up at 8 o'clock tomorrow morning to make a fast run to Ark. City. Will tell you about that later.

With all my love, Johnny

---

[1]   Curtis Street was renowned as a theater and entertainment district as early as the 1920's.

Refreshed and ready to move on, the young men left Wichita very early in order to arrive as scheduled in Arkansas City. The town anxiously awaited the group, excited from two newspaper articles announcing their trip before their arrival.

Arkansas City, Kansas (Pop. 12,903)

Like the state of Kansas and the local pronunciation of the Arkansas River, Arkansas City, Kansas is pronounced with the final 's', though it is often abbreviated as 'Ark City'. Located at the confluence of the Arkansas River and the Walnut River, the area served as an Indian settlement for centuries. Incorporated in 1872, by the turn of the century, Ark City rivaled Wichita for size and commerce.

Ark City is most famous for another sort of race: the Oklahoma Land Rush in 1893. At this time the Cherokee Strip was opened, offering 8,000,000 acres of land on a first-come basis. Ark City, only four miles north of the Oklahoma border where the race would start, grew from 5,000 to an estimated 150,000 people in the months before the land race started.

Ark City also developed as barge travel on the Arkansas River improved. Steamers carried up to 100,000 pounds of Kansas flour down to Fort Smith, the same route Johnny, Jerry, and Dick were following.

Thursday, June 30

Traveling from Wichita to Arkansas City meant a long, grueling day. Although it is only 63 miles by car, the river travel adds more than twenty miles to the distance. Aware of a grand reception awaiting them in Arkansas City, the trio pushed hard. A reporter from the Denver Post stated in a July 1st article, "They set a record of fourteen hours for the eighty five mile trip here from Wichita."

The people of Arkansas City were overwhelmingly enthusiastic in welcoming the adventurers. Crowds lined up on the Chestnut Avenue Bridge to watch for them. The police chief, Paul Lesh, had officers on hand to meet them at the river and drive them around the city. The owner of a nearby garage offered them its use to stow their gear while they were in town. After their tour of the city, the

44

hotel manager, H. S. McCurley, treated them to steak dinners at the Osage Hotel Grill with the police chief and Mayor E. S. Berry. William Walton, manager of the Burford theater, took them to a show after dinner, and even gave them stage time to tell about their trip so far. Johnny wrote about their arrival late that night:

June 30, posted July 1
Arkansas City, Kansas
(Osage Hotel- Boss Hotel Chain)

Dearest Berniece,
        This is an explanation of the last letter. You probably didn't understand it, well neither did I. It was written at about 1 o'clock in the morning and I had to get up at 3 o'clock so that explains part of it. While we were in Wichita, we received an invitation from the Arkansas City Chamber of Commerce. We got up at 3 o'clock, left Wichita at 4:30, and paddled 14 1/2 hours to get here. It was really rough. I could hardly walk or move my arms and the other guys were the same. Anyway as we came into the city limits we noticed a large crowd of people on the main bridge. So we stopped and tied up. We were met by the chief of Police, a large crowd, reporters, etc. They gave us a ride and a police escort into town where we were given a couple of small hotel rooms and introduced to the Mayor, more people, the manager of the hotel, the owner and manager of the newspaper, a theatre manager, and many others. Then we were the guests of honor at a steak dinner where we were served by the Mayor, chief of Police, and Hotel Manager. After that, we were the guests of the theatre manager who took us to a movie. Tomorrow we are to be shown the town by the Mayor and chief of Police, have a radio broadcast and more newspapers. Big wheels, huh? We are having lots of fun though and people are really swell.

Just in case you have forgotten - I love you. If you can find time, please write Tulsa, Okla. I really look forward to your letters.

With all my love my darling,

Johnny

The first remaining diary entry begins on July 1, in Arkansas City, Kansas.

Friday, July 1

We woke at 8:30 and had good breakfast at the Hotel Osage coffee shop. Radio station called and we went over there at 10:00. Met radio Station KSOK who gave us an interview over the air. Very interesting. Then the Police Chief and Mr. Wm Walton took us around the town and showed the local sights. At 12:20 we left Arkansas City with deep regrets. It was the most elaborate and the best organized reception we have received. Traveled fast until 6:00 then so exhausted from the previous day's work that we drifted with the slow deep current until 7:00 then ate a big dinner and went to bed early.

Steaks Too! Three Denver university students, canoeing from Pueblo, Colo., to New Orleans get a hearty welcome in Arkansas City, Kan., after their 80-mile trip from Wichita. Left to right are Mayor E. S. Berry, Dick Henke, chief of police, Paul Lesh, Jerry Pankow, hotel manager H. S. McCurley, and Johnny Evert. The boys are traveling in two canoes, and plan to return to Denver on motorcycles. (Photo and caption, originally published on July 1, 1949, reprinted by permission of *The Arkansas City Traveler.*)

47

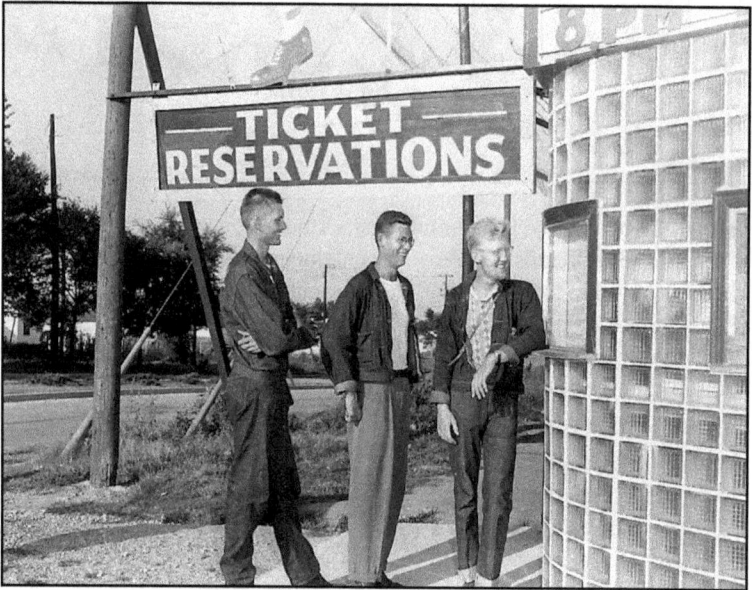

Dick, Johnny, and Jerry enjoyed going to the movies in many of the towns they visited along the way, often courtesy of the theater or town. In this snapshot, the city is not identified.

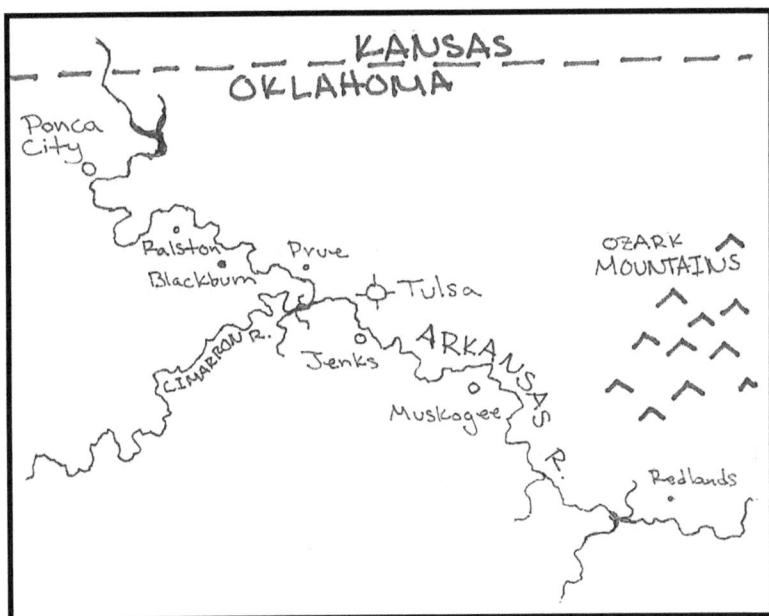

Missing: One Canoe

July 2 to July 11
Ponca City, Oklahoma to Muskogee, Oklahoma

Ponca City, Oklahoma (Pop. 20, 180)

Ponca City was named for the Ponca Tribe, who had originally come from the Great Plains and had been removed to Indian Territory in 1877-1878. The settlement remained part of Indian Territory until the 1893 land rush opened up the Cherokee Strip to white settlers, robbing the Ponca of much of their land. In spite of these incursions, Ponca culture remains strong even today.

The town of New Ponca was laid out in 1893. For several years, Ponca competed with nearby Cross, Oklahoma to attract the railroad and eventually won, leaving Cross to disappear. New Ponca remained part of Oklahoma Territory until 1907 when Oklahoma became the 46th state. The city was renamed Ponca City in 1913.

Johnny found the people of Ponca City very friendly and

welcoming. As eager to greet them as Arkansas City had been, the people of Ponca City were even more excited. The travelers planned to get to Ponca City by evening of July 1st, but that proved to be too ambitious. Worried by the delay, the Ponca City CAS station sent out a plane to find them. When the pilot spotted their camp, he wobbled the plane's wings to ask when they would arrive. In the days before cell phones and instant communication, writing in the sand worked just as well to let the citizens of Ponca City know when to expect the canoes.

Saturday, July 2
Woke at 5 AM. Broke camp at 5:45 and headed for Ponca City. Had a slow current. At 12:00 we stopped for lunch and a short swim. We just got out and Jerry and I dressed when an airplane buzzed us. John grabbed a poncho and wrapped himself up in it. We wrote in the sand that we would arrive in Ponca City at 1:00 pm and were only 7 minutes late. We were met by the Police Chief and the President of the Chamber of Commerce and some reporters. We ate steak at 1:30 and looked over the town and went swimming at the Conoco Refinery Gymn a most Beautiful building. We got out of the pool so late that we decided to see a movie in town and not shove off till morning. We saw Dear To My Heart (for free) and then met my reporter friend and went to the news office to get the first paper that came off the presses for Sunday morning. Oh yes- they even blew the siren in the police car when they drove us through town. Went to bed at 12:00.

Normally they really enjoyed having the airplanes buzz them. Back in Colorado, one plane had followed them for two days, but clearly this time they weren't expecting the pilot to surprise them skinny dipping.

After the impromptu parade with dozens of people greeting them and celebrating their arrival, Bob Dellinger of the local newspaper showed them the highlights. Prominent townsfolk were more than generous in offering the travelers their hospitality. Con-
50

Impressive Monument -- The three Denver canoeists who are paddling down the Arkansas river from Colorado to New Orleans pause during their stopover here Saturday to admire the Pioneer Woman statue made by sculptor Bryant Baker. The three were deeply impressed by the monument. The travelers are, left to right, Johnny Evert, Dick Henke, and Jerry Pankow. They were expected to arrive in Tulsa Wednesday. (Photo and caption, originally published in the Ponca City News on July 6, 1949, reprinted by permission, *Ponca City News.*)

tinental Oil Co. along with Chamber of Commerce president Frank Overstreet and member H. L. Schall, opened the gleaming Conoco Refinery Pool for them. Johnny later recalled that they were the only people swimming at the pool that day and had the whole, huge pool to themselves. All three were excellent swimmers and spent much of the time in the pool racing underwater. Tall and lean, Dick tanned evenly. Jerry was very blond and perpetually sunburned, especially his face. Johnny was tanned as brown as an oak. With his dark, curly hair and deep tan, he was a dark as any Black man he met.

After a complimentary steak dinner with their hosts from the chamber of commerce, Dick, Jerry, and Johnny went as guests of the management to the movies at the Poncan theater. They spent the night in a room in the Jens-Marie Hotel as guests of the hotel owner, J. J. Young, and spoke to the reporters the next day. Though they had fallen into a routine of paddling, swimming, camping, and greeting people, the young men talked about how much variety there was in river travel. No two days were alike, each bringing its own surprises and challenges.

The heat started to really sap their energy here. The further south they went, and the hotter it got, the harder it was to paddle in the mid-day sun. They tried getting up early and resting or swim-

51

ming in the hottest part of the afternoon, They also tried paddling at night but Dick hit a tree and nearly wrecked the canoe on some rocks, so they tied up after dark each night to camp on sandbars. During the day, biting flies troubled them. At night, mosquitoes whined in their ears and feasted on exposed skin while the river meandered lazily through cornfields and pastures. But slow travel and bothersome insects were not the only problem.

Sunday, July 3

About 8:30 this morning as we were packing to leave town we discovered that our two 22. Cal rifles were missing. We called the police at once and tried to trace them. Stolen in Wichita we believe. Left town at 9:15 and made a good run but got nowhere. The river winds too much. We were tired so tried drifting. It doesn't work. Made camp at 7:00 above Ralston and to bed.

Ralston, Oklahoma (Pop. 416)

Ralston was established in 1894 on the Atchinson, Topeka and Santa Fe railroad line, and at one time rivaled Tulsa for commercial promise. During Oklahoma's boom years at the turn of the century, many towns of the old west erected impressive buildings for multiple purpose use. Ralston boasts one such odd combination in the Ralston Opera House and Hardware. Built by the Harry Brothers in 1902, the theater and opera house is on the second floor, while the hardware store is housed below. The opera house was converted to a movie theater in the 1920's. The hardware store continued in operation until the 1970's. Efforts have been made to list the building on the National Register of Historic Places and to renovate it. Johnny, Dick, and Jerry undoubtedly saw the 50 x 80 foot native sandstone building when they napped in town, still trying to avoid heavy paddling during the heat of the day.

Monday, July 4

Started early after a good but damp sleep. Made Ralston about noon and slept a couple of hours in town then pushed on until

52

5:00 and made an early camp and shot off a couple of fire-crackers to celebrate the 4th. One can of beer per man made it a pleasant evening. To bed early for a good run tomorrow. To-night we decided to get some more guns in Tulsa. We almost stepped on a snake and it startled us a little bit. [Lost] the guns.

They had hoped to reach Tulsa by Independence Day because they had friends waiting to celebrate with them there, but they didn't make it. Instead they spent the holiday on a quiet sandbar with only the fish and snakes to notice the firecrackers.

Dick wrote:

Dear Uncle Bill, Aunt Ena, & Allen,
Man is this trip a killer.
I sure wish I was home sometimes.
Sent 2nd roll of movie film in today.
Tell Mom & Pop how the film came
out so we can improve the technique
used. I'll call them in a few days
again (The schmoo in OK but is dirty)
write in Tulsa Okla.
As Ever,
Dick

Blackburn. Oklahoma (Pop. 135)

Located on the south bank of the Arkansas River at a natural ford, Blackburn had a post office established as early as 1893, and was incorporated as a town in 1909. For a long time, Blackburn was a 'whiskey' town, which meant it was legal to sell alcohol there - an important distinction for the town since it bordered the 'dry' Indian Territory. Unfortunately, since the railroad never came through Blackburn, and no state highway was built there, the town failed to prosper. By the beginning of the 21st century, the population had dwindled to 102.

The first thing the canoeists saw as they came up to Black-burn was an impressive six-span Parker through-truss bridge, built in 1928. Johnny, Dick, and Jerry tied up by the bridge and restocked their supplies. They were behind schedule and running low on both food and water. The hard work of paddling meant they were always hungry. An adequate water supply was even more important since the river water was not drinkable. Stopping at small towns along the way helped keep them well supplied.

Tuesday, July 5

Got up early and had a very weak breakfast. Ran out of pancake flour and cereal. Had enough for only 4 people to use and 1 cup of cereal. Dick was not too hungry but Jerry and Johnny opened the last loaf of bread and ate it. Still hungry. We were not too far from the little town of Blackburn so we made a fast run there to pick up water and food. Made it in one hour and after stocking up with 6 gallons of water and $5 worth of groceries said goodbye to the swell people we met there and took off. Made a good run and a short stop for lunch. Had a race with a rain cloud all afternoon and finally we lost. As the rain was coming down pretty heavy we made camp. We had a good supper of 13 ears of corn, 3 potatoes, 3 cans of sauerkraut, 12 cups of chocolate and 6 wieners. Then to bed.

When the river ran through farmland, the young men often helped themselves to some of the sweet corn growing near the river-banks. Roasted on a campfire, the corn on the cob made a refreshing treat after a diet of canned beans and sauerkraut. Another occasional treat was a farmhouse meal. The kids fishing on the river would see the canoeists and run and tell the family. The farmers would call the newspaper down and invite them all in for a meal.

Prue, Oklahoma (Pop. unavailable for 1950, 465 in 2010)

The town of Prue, named for local landowner Henry Prue, was established in 1905 on an extension of the Missouri, Kansas and Oklahoma Railroad. Notable travelers through the area before Johnny, Dick, and Jerry included Washington Irving in 1832 and Nathaniel Boone in 1843. Irving wrote about the area in his book, *A Tour on the Prairies*. This area of Oklahoma between the Cimarron River and Arkansas River, bordered by the Osage Reservation and the Creek Reservation, was known as the Triangle Country. The wild, untamed hills riddled with caves made it an ideal hideout for outlaws including the famous Dalton Gang and Bill Doolin.

The current site of Prue, sometimes called New Prue, is north of the original site, which was inundated by the creation of Keystone Dam and Keystone Lake in 1968. The canoeists in 1949 had planned the trip mostly from aerial maps, which showed just how tangled the Arkansas River was, bending and twisting so much that as they traveled essentially south and east, they went north and west almost as much. Johnny thought they could probably make better time walking! They were going about six miles an hour, which was close to twice the speed of the current in that area. Unfortunately, the maps were not completely accurate. A new bridge had been built in 1948, and the bridge near Prue, shown on their maps, was no longer there. Without an accurate map, and with so many backwaters and bends, it is surprising they weren't lost more often. In this case, they reached Tulsa two days after they had planned their arrival.

Wednesday, July 6

A very bad night. Stormed all night and tent leaked. Got up at about 7:30. Everything was wet including sleeping bags. Left at 9:15. We looked for dam Bridge at Prue, OK but found out that the maps were wrong and they were no longer there. We were pretty worried until we saw the Cimarron River and got straightened out. We arrived in Tulsa, Okla. at 2:35 pm and were greeted by police and reporters. More pictures and a shower at the police station. Then we purchased 3 pistols since snakes have been giving us a bad time. Then a meal (free) at University of Tulsa and a bed out there for the night after a good ball game at the park.

The 11th Street Bridge crosses the Arkansas River in Tulsa. Built in 1916 and widened in 1929, the bridge became part of the famous cross-country Route 66, built in 1926. The bridge was used until 1972, and is currently closed to all traffic. (Photo from the Beryl Ford Collection/ Rotary Club of Tulsa, Tulsa City-County Library and Tulsa Historical Society.)

Tulsa, Oklahoma (Pop. 182,740)

First settled by the Muskogee (Creek) Indians from 1828 to 1836 after they were forced from their homeland in the southeast. Tulsa was part of Indian Territory. The Muskogee named it 'Tulasi,' meaning old town and having the same root as Talahassee, Florida, which was also named by the Muskogee. Tulsa, as it came to be known, grew as a trading town and prospered with the establishment of a post office there in 1879. The arrival of the railroad in 1882 brought more growth. By 1892, this part of Indian Territory was opened for white settlement and the Indians were forced to give up their tribal lands and take allotments. The town was incorporated in 1898. The oil boom of the early 20th century brought more change to Tulsa, transforming the tumultuous cowtown to an oil boomtown.

This snapshot taken from the road west of Tulsa provides a panoramic view of the broad sweep of the Arkansas River with flat plains on the left bank and rolling hills rising on the right bank.

Thursday, July 7
Got up after good night's sleep and ate at Univ. Went to Post Office for mail and sent some letters. Went to News Office (Indian letter). Went swimming at Y. Left at 5:00. Made camp at 6:30. Rained all night.

The News Office mentioned in the diary entry probably refers to the *Tulsa World*, which had absorbed the early major Tulsa newspaper called the *Indian Republican* sometime after 1907. In 1941, *Tulsa World* entered a joint operating agreement with *Tulsa Tribune*, and both continued publishing until 1992 when *Tulsa World* acquired *Tulsa Tribune*'s assets. So in 1949 both newspapers were operating, but only one interviewed the travelers.

In spite of continued heat, unpredictable rain, swift currents, and difficult bridges, Dick, Jerry, and Johnny were enjoying themselves. The reception in Tulsa kept them too busy to write much, but Dick managed a postcard home.

Dear Mom, Pop and Bob,
    We are really having a good time now in town. There always seems to be a reception committee awaiting our arrival. We leave Tulsa Okla today and push on. Write me in Little Rock Arkansas. Thanks for the cookies & pickles and am glad you like the cigars Pop. Newsreels may join in with us very soon but can't be sure
(Is it cool in Colo?)
    Love Dick

Jenks, Oklahoma (Pop. 1,037)

Now considered a suburb of Tulsa, Jenks came to the stage a bit later than some other towns along the Arkansas River. Established in 1904 and platted in 1905, Jenks owed its initial growth to the building of the railroad from Tulsa to Muskogee. Although both river and rail traffic contributed to Jenks' prosperity, the town was also important as a good river crossing. When the canoeists came through Jenks in 1949, they passed under the new two lane bridge built in 1948. Another boost to the economy in Jenks was the discovery of oil near Jenks in 1912, though unreliable water levels in the Arkansas and the constant threat of flooding especially in the 1920's and 1930's continued to cause problems. The new levee, built in 1948 just one year before Johnny, Dick, and Jerry arrived, helped control the flooding and protect the town.

Friday, July 8
    Slept late because it rained all night and traveled about 3 miles to Jenks. Mailed home letters and movie film and ate more ice cream bars while buying groceries. A local farmer

gave us about 15 lbs. of potatoes and we moved on. A bad snag caught John in the ribs when we crashed through some trees but he wasn't hurt too bad. Traveled till 8 o'clock. It started to rain again.

Years later Johnny had an x-ray showing that nearly all of his ribs had been broken at one time or another. He believes this may have been the first time he broke one of his ribs. But in his words, a broken rib is no big deal. He didn't even mention it in the letter to Berniece that he mailed from Jenks.

Dearest Berniece,
    Sorry I couldn't write from Tulsa but we were really cut short on our time. Had a wonderful reception there and were tied up most of the time. Please talk to Pastor Hansen about an appointment for me when I get back. I want to talk to him about a lot of things. Also find out if it will be possible for me to go on the 3 day outing.[1]–if so save a place for me. Darling I miss you more everyday and can hardly wait until I can get back. It's swell that you had a nice time at Estes Park. Will write again from Muskogee. Send mail to Little Rock.
    Love,
        Johnny

---

[1]   The 3 day outing Johnny mentions was sponsored by the Walther League, the youth group attached to St. John's Lutheran Church in Denver, through which Johnny had met Berniece. Johnny, a catholic, started participating with the Walther League because of his friendship with Dick, but he was not a member. This 3 day outing was a camping trip into the Rockies. Since Pastor Hansen was the pastor of St. John's, Johnny wanted to talk to him about what he had to do as a Catholic to marry Berniece, a Lutheran.

Muskogee (Pop. 37,289)

Muskogee started as a railtown in 1872 with the first rail line to cross Indian Territory, but the area had been a meeting place for Indians and fur traders long before that. The first permanent settlement was as early as 1817, though Muskogee was not incorporated as a city until 1898.

Situated just south of the confluence of the Arkansas River, the Verdigris River, and the Grand River, Muskogee sits at the edge of the oak and hickory forest region of Eastern Oklahoma and the prairies of the north-western part of the state. In the last part of the 19th century, it was the most important city in Indian Territory with the headquarters of the Union Agency for the 5 Civilized Tribes located there in 1875.

In 1905 the Indians of the area applied for admittance into the United States as the state of Sequoyah, with Muskogee as the capital. The application was denied, and Muskogee became part of Oklahoma Territory, joining the union with the rest of the state in 1907.

Saturday, July 9

Decided to get to Muskogee tonight and put in a good 8 hr day to reach there. It rained most of the day and so we traveled in swimsuits. Sky cleared about 3 and all 3 of us got bad sunburns on the legs. We landed at the old Highway #69 Bridge and pulled the boats way up on an island and started into town. We walked about a mile and finally got a ride in. Lucky we did since it's 7 miles from the river. Made arrangements for bed at the YMCA and went out to eat. Town on the whole seems rather unfriendly and is very poorly laid out and hard to find [your way] through. Pretty disgusted and drank 4 beers each and went to bed.

Unfriendly people and a poorly laid out town proved to be the least of their problems in Muskogee.

Sunday, July 10

Got up at 9:30 and all 3 of us went to church and met again at the YMCA. Ate breakfast and walked around town for an hour or so. Heard that they were running time trials for the soap box derby and walked over to see them. Met a fellow by the name of A. L. Buck who took us out to where we left the boats and arrived at the bridge to find 1 boat tied up to a tree and the other one gone completely.

We were completely horrified and didn't know what the score was until a lady living close to the river said that a boy had pulled in the blue boat first just as it started to drift free (WATER ROSE IN RIVER 8 to 10 in overnight) and hadn't seen the other. We needed quick action so Mr. Buck drove John and Dick out to the airport and took Jerry to the police station and sheriff's office where he contacted the newspaper, Radio stations, Highway Patrol, etc. Dick has a Pilots license and got checked out in a piper cub to fly over the river and see if we could find the boat. Just as John was about to get into the plane he was called to the phone and the police said they knew where the boat was. John and Dick got back into the car and went into town to find Jerry. Contacted Jerry at the YMCA and he told us that this fellow who found the boat about 5 miles downstream was going to claim salvage on it. So there goes most of the rest of our money, I guess. At times this trip really hurts and this is one of those times. Anyway we get the boat back tomorrow so we can be glad of that. We hope to lighten up our gear and travel much lighter. It gets so hot you would rather die then go on at times. Ate dinner and went to a cheap movie. All kind of worried about tomorrow and how much our boat will cost.

Monday, July 11

Got up around 8:30 and went to eat, then went to Post Office to get what mail was supposed to be there. Then went to an army store and got a pup tent. We decided to get rid of the big tent so as to lighten the load. Went to the highway and started to walk, got a ride just a half mile from the bridge all of us got in the one boat and went to the fellow's house downstream who has our second boat. After getting the equipment to the river we found that it was going to cost $15.00 for the guy pulling the boat out. As far as we are concerned Muskogee is no good. After getting the boat we shoved off for Ft. Smith. Traveled the rest of the day and did rather good. Still burned up about Muskogee. Made camp and ate. Had to put up the tent as the bugs were everywhere.

Years later, both Johnny and Jerry said the fellow who claimed salvage really stole the canoe, along with everything in it. The guy was a real barefoot hillbilly, wearing nothng but old overalls. He said the canoe had floated into his private pool, but Johnny, Dick, and Jerry didn't believe that. Although the sheriff helped them recover the boat, he was not much friendlier than the alleged thief. This part of the Arkansas River was where the flattened plains of the west rise into the foothills of the Ozark Mountains. Rolling and wooded, the area around here was very wild, with trees and bushes instead of farmland crowding the riverbanks. Johnny figured they were lucky they got the canoe back at all.

In most places, the local police, reporters and townsfolk were very help-ful to the canoeists. In the photos above and opposite, police officers help Johnny, Dick, and Jerry unload their gear and carry the canoes to a local garage or other secure 'parking' spot during their stay in the town.

Jerry, in the single canoe, and Dick and Johnny in the lead canoe, approach Fort Smith, Arkansas. Dick and Johnny had deep tans and went shirtless, but Jerry wore long sleeves and long pants in spite of the heat in order to avoid sunburn. The bridge seen here, built in 1922, was the 4th to span the Arkansas River. Called the Million Dollar Free Bridge, due to the cost of its construction, it was the first toll-free bridge crossing the Arkansas River from Fort Smith to Oklahoma. The bridge was replaced in the 1970's.

Van Buren
Redlands
Ozark
OZARK MOUNTAINS
Fort Smith
Morrilton
Dardanelle
ARKANSAS
ARKANSAS R.
Little Rock
OKLAHOMA
OUACHITA MOUNTAINS
Gillett
Pine Bluff
Yancopin
Watson
Arkansas City

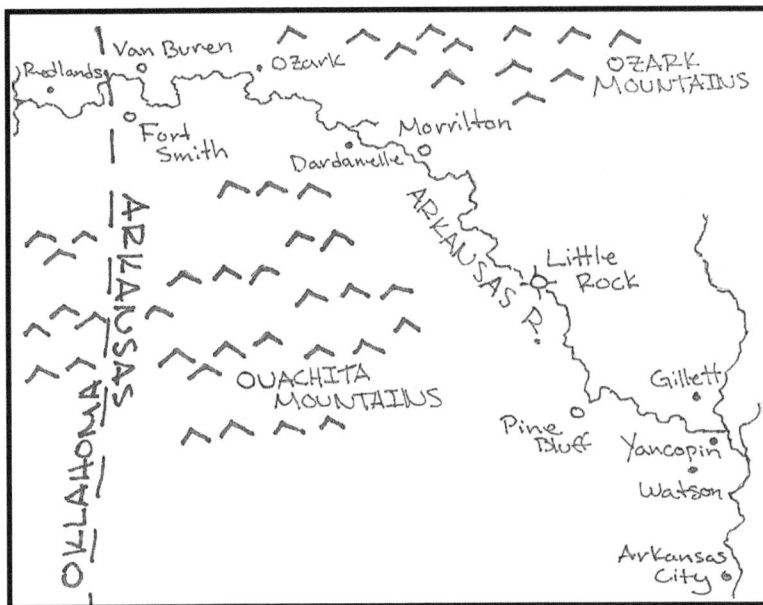

Through the Mountains and into the Delta

July 12 to July 27
Redlands, Oklahoma to the Mississippi River

Tuesday, July 12

Got up and ate and shoved off in pretty good time. Traveled till noon and found we had made 40 miles. Not too bad in the heat. Our food supply is almost gone and for the first time we find ourselves without much water. Didn't eat much tonight as we want to save what water we have for the morning meal. Got to bed earlier than ever for some time.

Johnny, Dick, and Jerry had hoped to supplement their food supply with fishing and hunting. In this they were unlucky. They never caught any fish, and the guns proved more useful for dealing with snakes than shooting anything worth eating.

They did shoot one wild meal. Johnny was paddling in the smaller canoe, and had his .22 close. A unlucky duck swam about 150 yards ahead of him. Johnny shot the duck in one eye, through the head, and out near the other eye. They retrieved the duck easily. Johnny, who knew how to clean and gut the duck from his butcher shop days, was ready to provide them with a feast. He boiled the prepared duck in a pot of water. But wild duck is kind of tough. So after boiling it, Johnny covered it with two or three inches of thick river mud. He covered some potatoes with the same kind of mud. Then he put the duck and potatoes in the fire and baked them until the mud was hard and dry. The young men cracked off the mud and ate. Johnny said, "The potatoes very good--the duck not so much. It was still mostly raw and gamy tasting, but we were hungry." They were still hungry and thirsty as they came to Redlands.

Redlands, Oklahoma (Pop. unavailable)

Currently a ghost town, Redlands was already practically unpopulated in 1949. Southeast of Gans, on the north bank of the Arkansas River, the site is archeologically important due to the prehistoric Spiro Mounds nearby. Unfortunately, the mounds were mostly looted a century ago.

The railroad crossed the Arkansas River at Redlands. The bridge was nine spans in a single track, or 2110 feet long. Legend has it that the original railroad bridge here was timber, and used by locals for their own purposes. The bridge was lost to flooding several times before flood control measures were put in place in the 1950's. Dick, Johnny, and Jerry found the bridge, but little else in Redlands.

If Redlands and Muskogee, the last two towns they mentioned in Oklahoma were disappointing, Fort Smith, Arkansas made up for it with a lavish welcome.

Fort Smith, Arkansas (Pop. 47,942)

Fort Smith, first built in 1817, lies on the Arkansas/Oklahoma border, where the Arkansas River and the Poteau Rivers join. Here the Arkansas River winds through a wide valley between the Ozark Mountains to the north and the Ouachita Mountains to the south. Set high on the bluffs called Belle Point, the fort's first mission was to keep the peace between the Osage and the Cherokee Tribes, negotiate treaties, and patrol the contested border between the United States and lands claimed by Spain. Its location on the edge of Indian Territory soon made it a key town in the settlement of the west and an important trading center. Although the army abandoned the fort in 1824 as the frontier shifted, they moved back to the fort in 1838 to assist with enforcing the Indian Removal Act. Meanwhile the civilian part of the town flourished. In 1858, Fort Smith was a major division center of the Butterfield Overland Mail.

The raucous frontier town of Fort Smith was finally brought to order under the famous "hanging judge," Isaac Parker. During his 21 year term, he sentenced 160 to death, though only 79 of them were actually hung.

Six years before Johnny, Dick, and Jerry came through Fort Smith in May, 1943, the Arkansas River at Fort Smith crested at 48'23", which was twenty feet above flood stage.

Wednesday, July 13

Got a good early start since we couldn't linger over the small breakfast that Dick prepared. Traveled about 3 hours and discovered that the town of Redlands which we were going to stop at was practically nonexistent. We pushed on and after about 4 hours were so hungry that we had to stop and used up our last box of pancake flour. Had to eat them dry for we have no other food. We finally saw the outskirts and the skyline of the famous town of Ft. Smith, Ark. We stopped and shaved and washed up then got to town at 4:15 and were greeted by Mr. Tom Ward, a real estate salesman who was fishing on the banks of the Ark. River for the 1st time. We were the total catch for the day. We had a nice long talk and he said he would guard the boats while we ate and looked over the town. An extremely well laid out town, clean and the people seem very friendly almost jovial. We were interviewed by the local newspapers, pictures and arrangements for a media broadcast which is scheduled for Thurs. Very busy but swell day. While Mr. Ward took us around town, Mr. Olen Anderson and Boy Scout Troop 6 were kind enough to help us out and watch the canoes. Went to bed at 11 o'clock after a wonderful day.

Van Buren, Arkansas (Pop. 6,413)

Northeast of Fort Smith, Van Buren sits on the north bank of the Arkansas River in the foothills of the Boston Mountains, which form the highest and most rugged portion of the Ozark Mountains. The first settlers arrived in 1818 and more followed. They called the place Phillips Landing after Thomas and Daniel Phillips, who built a lumber yard there to supply fuel for the river boat traffic. The town was renamed for the Secretary of State, Martin Van Buren, in 1831 when the post office was opened. Van Buren was incorporated in 1842. By 1857, Van Buren was a stop on the Butterfield Stage Route from Saint Louis to California. The first train to arrive in Van Buren was in 1876. Johnny, Dick, and Jerry stopped only briefly in Van Buren.

The old Frisco Railroad Bridge from Fort Smith to Van Buren was rebuilt after the flood of 1943 washed it away. Note the narrow passages between supports. (Photo by Doug Wertman)

Thursday, July 14

Had to get up early so the townspeople could not see us in the rain. Left the canoes in the care of some workmen in the vicinity and got the water bag filled up and had breakfast. Then we went back to the canoes. Tom Ward and a Mr. Terry Hill were there. Mr. Hill was to stay with the canoes while Tom Ward, a veteran of several tough campaigns in the Navy, was to take us around town. First out to station KFPW where we had a half hour broadcast. Met a Mr. Duke DuCoin, one fine guy. A Mr. W. E. Kunkel offered to fix our radio so while he was doing that we made another broadcast at station. We were interviewed by Johnny Trotter, a well known correspondent. After receiving three swell flashlights, the gift of Mr. DuCoin, we stocked up with food given us at a discount and then went over to the gigantic Wortz bakery where we had the pleasure of meeting the plant manager and Mr. Wortz the owner. A large well organized facility, they are famous over the country for their fine soda crackers. Received some wonderful cookies, biscuits and crackers there. Back to town where Mr. DuCoin bought us a steak dinner then with much regret we said goodby to the swell people of Ft. Smith and shoved off at 2:15. We traveled about an hour and came to the town of Van Buren Ark. to house of Bob Burns. Mr. Ward and his son Johnny were waiting for us

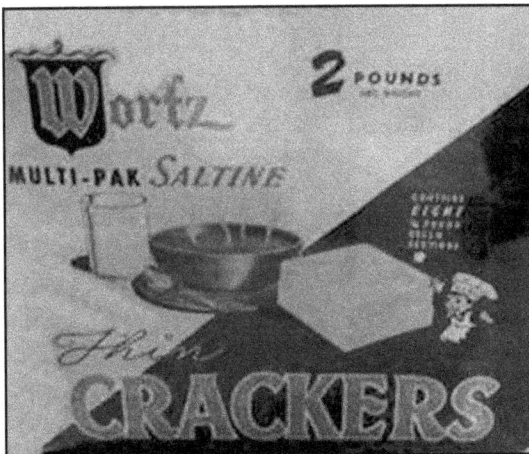

In 1903, Christian "Carl" H. Wortz Sr. and his wife moved their successful cracker company from Winchester, Indiana to Fort Smith, Arkansas, where it became the largest independent cracker and biscuit company in the Southwest, with the company slogan, "Biscuits that build."

at the bridge, taking pictures and we stopped and talked. Dick and John went into Van Buren for a case of beer while Jerry stayed with the boats. Had to go back across the county line. Van Buren was a dry county. Got the beer, said a last goodby to Mr. Ward and paddled for about two more hours. Made camp on a sand bar at 7:00 and after a supper of beans and crackers, drank some beer and listened to the Radio that we had been given by Mr. Kunkel who said it was useless to fix the small radio. We talked until about 9:00 then went to bed. Ft. Smith is a wonderful town with some of the finest people we have met so far. We are all surprised at the southern hospitality. Sure is different from Muskogee.

Van Buren, Arkansas is in Crawford County, whereas Fort Smith, Arkansas is in Sebastian County, Crawford was (and still is as of 2010) a dry county and Sebastian County is wet with dry areas. Wet and dry counties refer to the 'blue' laws restricting alcohol consumption and sales. In a wet county it is legal to buy alcohol; in a dry county it is not.

Traveling onward from Van Buren, the canoeists swept past the southern edge of Devils' Den State Park, established in the 1930's. Here the rugged and beautiful oak and hickory forests of the Ozark Mountains line the riverbank. Devil's Den State park includes a preserved section of the Butterfield stage route. During the Civil War, the area was riddled with hideouts for guerrilla troops from both sides of the conflict.

Along the north side of the Arkansas River, the Boston Mountains continue. This rocky mountain range is the highest between Appalachia and the Rockies. These rugged slopes are still mostly forested as part of the Ozark National Forest.

Ozark, Arkansas (Pop. 1,757)

The city of Ozark, Arkansas perches on the north bank of the Arkansas River at the northern most bend of the river in the state of Arkansas. The name, a simplification of the French 'Aux Arc' comes from the French explorers and means "at the big bend." The area was included in the Louisiana Purchase of 1803. By 1830, a settlement had grown at this important crossing of the Arkansas River. Steamboats carrying Indians west on the Trail of Tears stopped here when the river was too low to continue westward.

After all the hard work of the upper Arkansas, Dick, Jerry, and Johnny were ready for some relaxing travel. This was river life as it was meant to be. They had no prearranged contacts in Ozark, so the reception there surprised them.

Friday, July 15

We got up rather late this morning as we knew for sure that it would only take us a short time to get to Ozark, which was to be our next stop. We ate and then traveled till noon, when we stopped to eat. We had some sandwiches and drank beer and then decided to float in the current. So for the next three hours we drifted down the river drinking beer and listening to the radio. As we finished a can of beer Dick would sink it in the river by shooting at it. Once Dick decided he would open a can of beer by shooting a hole in it with his .22. He pulled the trigger when the gun was only 2 inches from the beer can. Beer flowed out each hole and he was covered with it. Finally arrived 3:00 we started to paddle so as to get to Ozark in time to get to the Post Office. We got to the bridge that went into Ozark and saw some people on the bridge. We tied the boats and had just got our boots on when a group of men broke through the underbrush and said hello. One of the men was a photographer so he took our picture. He then said "Mayor you get over and I'll take your picture with the young men." Were we ever surprised. So Mayor Harlon McClellan had his picture taken too. The mayor then took us into town. He got us a hotel room for the night and we were then taken to the home of Lt. Colonel Jack Paul. We stayed there and talked and were told about the region and had a very good time. Miss Ozark who was also Miss Arkansas Valley (Pat Moore) was also there and we felt honored. At 10:00

we went to the Wode Café and had dinner. Then we were taken to see Ozark's new ball field. It is one of the best lighted we have ever seen. We then went to the hotel and to bed.

Saturday, July 16

Got up at 8:00 and went to the café again. Mrs. McClellan was there and we talked while eating. We then went to the Post Office and mailed some letters and Dick called home. After that we went to see Mr. Anderson and he took us to the boats and we shoved off. It was 12:15 when we left. We paddled for some time and then saw some people on the bank. They got in a flat boat and came out to see us. It is the first time this has ever happened to us. Another boat coming over to see us. We paddled on till seven and saw on the map that we had gone quite a ways. Ate a good dinner and then to bed. Soup given us by Mrs. Anderson.

Jerry, Dick, and Johnny enjoyed eating at cafés whenever they were in town. The Wode Café in Ozark is the only one they mention by name.

72

Both Dick and Johnny mailed letters from Ozark.

Hi Mom & Pop & Bob,

    Still having a great time. Should arrive
Little Rock on Thurs. Guests of Mayor of Ozark
last night. River getting faster (Thank goodness)
I'll be sending my little Radio home to be fixed
soon. Fort Smith gave us a new portable and
batteries the other day. How's fishing Bob? Let's
hear from you. Have you used the kayak[1] yet?

    Love ,
        Dick

July 16 Ozark, ARK
Dearest Berniece,

    Been pretty lonesome but the local
Southern belles have been very friendly.
Everyone has been swell with the exception
of Muskogee. Getting darker every day but
not sunburned as yet. Slowly gaining weight
but it is a tough process. I eat too much
and it costs money. Lost one of the canoes
at Muskogee and it cost $15.00 to get it back.
Think you could negotiate a small loan of about
$50.00? What's the deal with Pastor Hansen
about the 3 day outing?[2] Also what's the date
of our Wedding? Could you meet me in New
Orleans on the 16th of Aug? If so, pack
your bags and let me know where.

    All my Love, Johnny

---

[1]   Dick is referring to one of the kayak kits he had purchased from
Sears for the trip, but ended up giving to his brother instead.

[2]   For an explanation of the three day outing see page 59. At this
point Johnny has hinted at marriage several times, and even asks Berniece
about it in this letter, but she has not accepted.

Dardanelle, Arkansas (Pop. 1,772)

Dardanelle, situated about halfway between Fort Smith and Little Rock, was an important transportation center throughout the 19th century with hundreds of barges and other boats passing through annually. The town was incorporated in 1855 though it had been settled for over twenty years, making it one of the oldest towns in Arkansas. The scenic area surrounding Dardanelle is now known for fishing, birding, and other outdoor activities. For Johnny, Dick, and Jerry, the barges in Dardanelle marked the first signs they were approaching the Mississippi River.

Sunday, July 17

Got up early and as usual broke camp late; almost 9:45 traveled very fast for three hours and made 20 miles. Came to the town of Dardanelle, stopped at the bridge and went into town. We saw our first barge -tugs, a type of river boat. We are happy to note that we can get the radio station from New Orleans and the tugs were from the Port of Memphis. In Dardanelle we ate an excellent meal and saw a show. Left town at 5:00 traveled for two hours and made camp. Good meal and went to bed.

A view of the Arkansas River, looking north from the eastern end of Petit Jean State Park in Conway County, Arkansas. (Photo by Photolitherland - Chris Litherland, at en.wikipedia (http://en.wikipedia.org))

Morrilton, Arkansas (Pop. 5,483)

In 1820, Major William Lewis and his son settled in the area approximately one mile south of the present day town of Morrilton. By 1825 they had established a trading post. Incorporated in 1844, the place was called Lewisburg. When tracks were laid through the valley in 1871, the railroad bought land from E. J. Morrill, calling the area Morrilton. Gradually people shifted from Lewisburg to Morrilton to be closer to the railroad. Lewisburg was abandoned by 1880 and the depot at Morrilton was built in 1910.

Coming down the river from Ozark to Morrilton, the canoeists would have passed the scenic Petit Jean Mountain. This mesa, 1,000 feet above the Arkansas River Valley stretches about five miles west to east along the south bank of the Arkansas River, nineteen miles west of Morrilton. Petit Jean State Park was established around this towering rocky bluff in 1923. On the north bank opposite Petit Jean Mountain lies rich river-bottom farmland.

Monday, July 18
Awake at 6:00 and started out at 8:00. Decided to float since we were not too far from Morrilton. Floated for 4 hours and paddled for 2 more arrived at 4 p.m. and at 4:45 were taken into town by jeep by the local game warden. Were interviewed by the press and started out hitting the soda fountain. Dick had 2 melts and a chocolate soda and got sick from it. Purchased a half a gal of wine to drink that evening. Walked back 3 miles to boats and moved downstream 5 miles where we spent the evening eating and drinking wine.

The wine was a mistake. They didn't get far the next day.

Tuesday, July 19
BAD DAY. 3 hangovers. We didn't drink wine anymore. Shoved off at 8 p.m. for some night travel but after hitting a log and narrowly missing a large rock we landed on a sand bar and hit the sack. Very uncomfortable.

75

Pinnacle Mountain, as seen from the Natural Steps on the Arkansas River, was an important landmark long before 1819, when naturalist Thomas Nuttal wrote about it. Just west of Little Rock, the mountain is part of the Ouachita Mountain Range. Although not established as a state park until 1977, the mountain would have been easily visible from the river in 1949. (Photo by BartLIV)

Little Rock, Arkansas (Pop. 102,213)

Little Rock, the largest city in Arkansas, is located in the foothills of the Ouachita Mountains. With Quapaw lands to the south and Osage lands to the north, there was a settlement of mixed French and Indians families on the south bank of the Arkansas River as early as 1769. Even before that, in 1721, French explorers named the area 'La Petite Roche' (Little Rock) and counted it as a well known river crossing, opposite the 'big rock' bluff across the river. In 1803, the Louisiana Purchase, including Little Rock and the surrounding area, transferred the land from the French to the United States. Though it was a small wilderness town in 1819 when Arkansas became a territory, Little Rock's location near the center made it ideal for a the capital. In 1821, Little Rock replaced Arkansas Post as the territorial capital and remained the capital when Arkansas became a state in 1836. Arkansas joined the Confederacy in 1861, but Little Rock was occupied by Union Troops in 1863. Reconstruction following the war was devastating for the Southern states, including Arkansas. In Little Rock, the conflict between the scalawags and carpetbaggers erupted in violence in 1874 in the Brooks-Baxter War over the gubernatorial election. President Grant eventually intervened and declared Baxter the governor, thus ending the conflict.

By 1949, at least six bridges crossing the Arkansas River in Little Rock connected the north and south banks. As Johnny, Dick, and Jerry came into Little Rock shooting underneath each of those bridges, the water was pretty rough, coming to within a quarter of an inch of the rim of the canoe.

Wednesday, July 20

Up at 5 a.m. Ate hearty breakfast of Malt.O.Meal, pancakes, etc. Packed extra pancakes for lunch and left at 6:15. At 11 a.m. we were buzzed by a P-51 mustang and got some beautiful pictures (I hope)[3]. John had 1 foot in the water just in case the pilot got any closer. Stopped at 1:00 PM and packed our laundry and cleaned up for Little Rock. Found a small road house and grocery store just off the river 1/2 mile and talked to the proprietor for quite a while. Left there at 2 and pushed on to Little Rock. We turned the last bend before going into town and met some very high waves (almost swamped). A tiny boat was pushing a sand barge downstream and when they saw us they hailed us over. We tied up to the tug and they took us into town where the reporters and radio young men were gathered. We met the mayor of Little Rock and he drove us over to the YMCA where we were to spend the night. The mayor said that the mayor of New Orleans was a friend of his and he'd give us a letter to take to him. (good deal) Went swimming at the YMCA then dinner and went to the movie. Retired in a real bed at 11:30 quite tired.

---

[3]   These pictures have not survived.

Thursday, July 21

We got up this morning and went down stairs to await our radio program. We were listening to the last of the program when the reporter came from the Arkansas Democrat and we gave him what information he wanted. Jerry went to call the Mayor about getting a ride to the Post Office. He found that the fire chief was to pick us up at the front of the Y. The reporter took some pictures and then the Chief of the Fire Dept. came and took us to the P.O. He then took us to a place to get our laundry done. Later he took us around to see the town. What a town, really nice. After this we decided to see a show. Then we went to the Y and took another swim. After swimming Marshall Hendrix met us and we were taken to a grocery store where we got a lot of food to take with us. We then went to dinner and had two dinners apiece. Hungry. Then to bed. Radio talk for way to get home.

One reason for the additional radio program was to set up a sponsorship for their trip home. Although the program garnered a lot of attention, no sponsorship developed. Not only were the canoeists trying to raise funds, local businesses, such as the Cavalier Cigarette Company, used the popularity of the canoe trip for advertising purposes. Cavalier cigarettes were first introduced in 1949 by the Reynolds Tobacco Company, so these were a brand new product at the time.

Johnny, Dick, and Jerry really enjoyed the attention they received in Little Rock and the chance to catch up on news. They were momentarily stunned at the post office in Little Rock, when Jerry asked for mail, and the clerk said there was nothing there for him. He did find a single letter for Dick. Then someone realized these were the guys on the river. It turned out, the postal workers had been waiting for them and had three whole bundles of mail, including packages and letters tied up with a string. Unfortunately, some of the news they got from potential sponsors in Little Rock was disheartening. Dick wrote:

Hi folks,

Well everything blew up in our
faces. Motorcycle deal fell through,
Arkansas Valley Journal doesn't want more
articles and John is just about broke.
Write to us in Vicksburg, Miss.
We leave Little Rock in an hour at 9:00
after broadcast. Call KTLN and ask
about a program being sent up
from Little Rock also. The Everts
might record it if you ask them.

Love, Dick

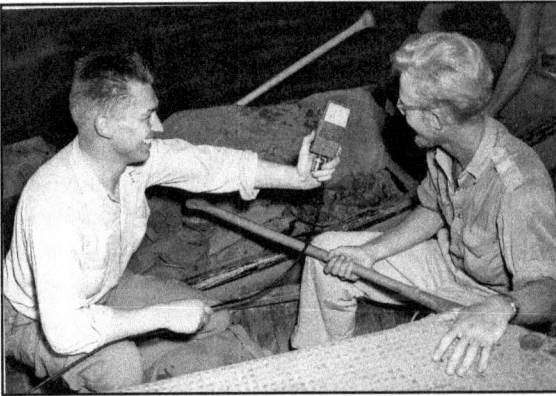

In many towns, the canoeists were interviewed by the local radio station. The unidentified radio announcer in these photos talked to the travelers before they left the canoes. In Little Rock, Marshall Hendrix of radio station KVLC was one of the radio announcers. Top: Jerry (right) tells the radio audience his impressions of the trip so far. Below: John (left) and Jerry (right) listen while Dick (center) speaks with the announcer. (Photo by Johnnie Gray, © *Arkansas Gazette*, Little Rock, Arkansas. July 24, 1949.)

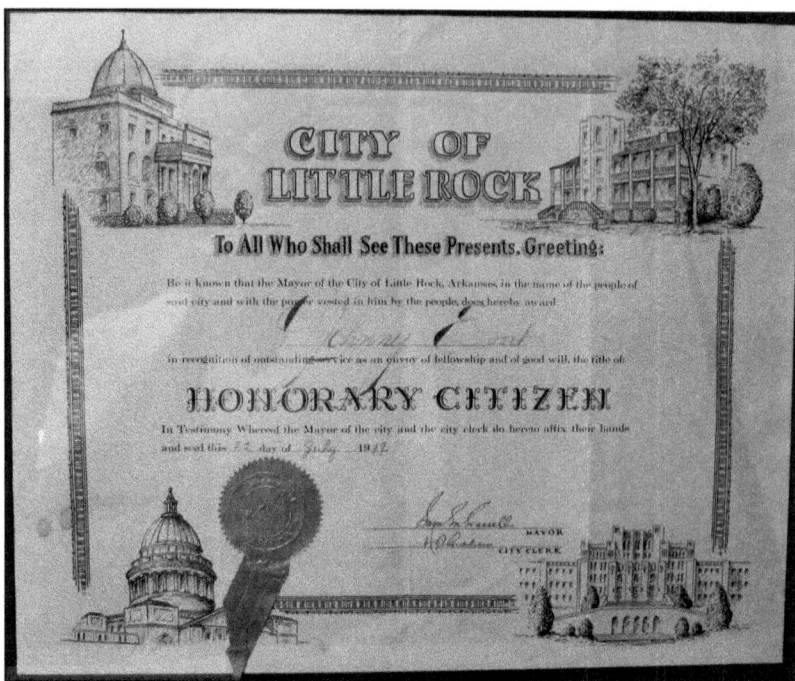

Sam M. Wassell, the mayor of Little Rock in 1949, wrote a letter of introduction to the mayor of New Orleans, DeLesseps Story "Chep" Morrison. Wassell also made the three young men honorary citizens of Little Rock.

Friday, July 22

    Got up real early 6:45 and met Marshall in the lobby of the Y. He took us to eat and then we went to the boats. While we were getting everything ready to go Marshall told us what we were to do while the program was going on. The Mayor came and also the owner of the grocery store. A man came from the Cavalier Cigarette Company. When the program began the three above mentioned men presented us with the various items. The Mayor made us Honorary Citizens of Little Rock. After this we went to the boats and said a few words to our radio audience. Then the radio program was over. We stood around and chatted with everyone and Jerry let the radio manager use his camera to get some pictures. We shoved off at 9:30 think highly of the many people we had met. We paddled till 12:00 and then ate a loaf of bread and sat around talking for a while before going on again. We paddled on and the further we went the harder the wind blew till finally the wind was really raising waves. We decided to halt then because it's too hard work to paddle. We camped and thought of getting to Pine Bluff sometime after noon. Which meant we would have to lay over till Monday. Rained all night.

Pine Bluff, Arkansas (Pop. 37, 162)

As the river reaches Pine Bluff, it leaves the Arkansas timber region, and enters the delta region. The timber region is hilly terrain with dense pine and cypress forests. The delta region is flatter, with wide fields and farmlands, full of creeks, streams, and bayous. Just northwest of Pine Bluff is the northern-most point of Bayou Bartholomew, the longest bayou in the world, winding some 364 miles south into Louisiana. Bayou Bartholomew is the ancient channel for the Arkansas River, dumping into the Ouachita River instead of the Mississippi River.

When Europeans arrived in the Pine Bluff area, the Quapaw were the main people living there. In 1819 Joseph Bonne, of mixed Quapaw and French blood, settled on the pine-covered bluff overlooking the Arkansas River. The high ground helped keep the settlement safe from intermittent flooding. The town was incorporated in 1839 with 50 residents. By 1860, it was the area of the largest slave holdings in Arkansas, and cotton cultivation built the county's wealth.

Pine Bluff has always depended on the river for traffic and trade, but the course of the Arkansas River has always been fickle. Just west of Pine Bluff lies Lake Langhofer, a natural oxbow lake, formed long ago when the Arkansas River main channel shifted. The lake provides Pine Bluff with a natural slackwater harbor, and later levees built along the river have helped prevent the main channel from shifting more, but the area is still full of backwaters and confusing channels.

Even though the young men were experienced canoeists by now, the Arkansas River remained unpredictable. A violent rainstorm blew up as they neared Pine Bluff, nearly swamping them.

Dick expected a set of fencing swords to arrive in Pine Bluff so he could keep in practice for the fencing team at Denver University. No one remembers now if the fencing swords arrived, and if so, how Dick could practice along the way.

Saturday, July 23

Got up and ate and emptied the water from the rain out of the boats shoved off at 9:30. Paddled and for the first time on the trip we didn't know where we were. The winds came up again but we kept on going. Got to Pine Bluff and tied up next to some river tugs. We are getting into a bigger & deeper river. A man by the name of Charles White took us into town and left us at the News Paper Office. We were interviewed and a radio man got in touch with us. We appeared on another radio program. We got a hotel room and ate 5 hamburgers. While [we were] eating, the Secretary of the Chamber of Commerce called and invited us to the Oakland Club for dinner and dancing. We accepted. We went to the radio station and then to the club. What a night. Had dinner (steak) and danced with some girls we were introduced to. In the middle of the dance we were presented to the audience. Made us feel real good. Then to the hotel and to bed.

Beer Beer Beer

Jerry had 14   Dick had 12   Johnny had 14

Sunday, July 24

Got up real late. Hangovers. (Jerry) Went to eat and then got some of the things we needed. String, glue for boat seat which broke. Shoved off at 12:30 and paddled till 6:00. Worked on seat and got everything straightened out. Ate and listened to radio, then to bed.

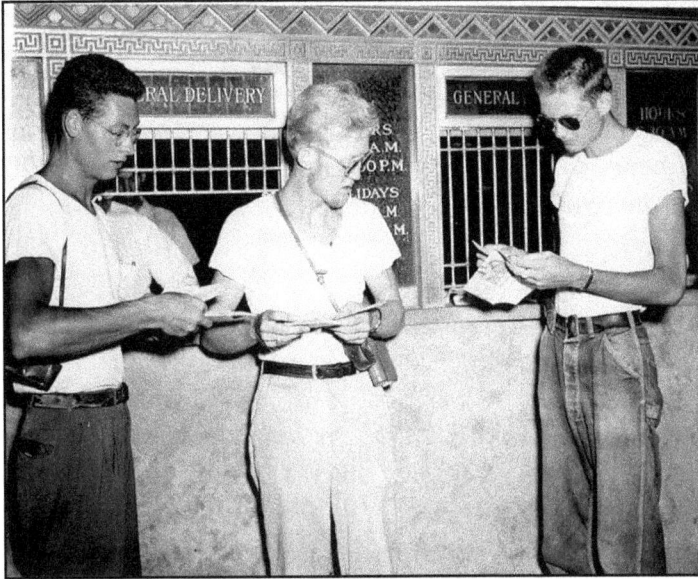

Johnny, Jerry, and Dick enjoyed hearing from folks back home and checked for mail care of general delivery at each post office.

Gillett, Arkansas (Pop. 774) - Pendleton Ferry

Leaving Pine Bluff, the river continues to spread across the delta flowing mostly eastward. This was an untamed river, muddy and full of treacherous currents. The Arkansas River of the delta region teems with wildlife: turtles, frogs, waterfowl of all types, and of course, alligators. The canoeists still camped on sandbars, but spent less time swimming in the river.

The area is heavily agricultural. Gillett was founded on this rich river bottom land. The first white settlers, mostly of German origin, arrived in 1881. The town was platted in 1888, and the railroad arrived in 1895. Sawmills, the timber industry and farming were the mainstays for the town's economy.

The Pendleton Ferry crossed the Arkansas River between Pendleton and Arkansas Post. Today, Pendleton is listed as a populated place in Desha County. Population estimates for 1949 are not available. Arkansas Post was the first European settlement in Arkansas, with the first post established there in 1686. Arkansas Post served as the first capital of Arkansas Territory, but the community died when the capital was moved to Little Rock. Currently, Arkansas Post is a National Monument. The Pendleton Ferry remained in operation until the early 1970's when it was replaced by a bridge. At one time, Arkansas had more ferries than bridges, but by 2000, only one of the Arkansas River ferries remained.

Monday, July 25

Got up later than usual at 9:30, had our regular hearty but leisurely breakfast, and shoved off at 11:50. Twenty minutes after we left we were lost and stayed that way most of the day. Made excellent time, as we discovered when we landed at the Pendleton Ferry below (South) of Gillett. Got there at 6:30 and made camp immediately after leaving there. Had a ride across the river on the ferry—our first ferry ride on the Ark. River.

Yancopin, Arkansas (Pop. unavailable)

Yancopin is listed as a populated place in Desha County, Arkansas. The Yancopin Bridge (pronounced YAN ki pin) was built in 1903 for the Missouri-Pacific Railway and kept in use until 1992. At over a mile long, with trestles attached to both the north and south ends, this bridge is one of the longest in Arkansas, and is probably the longest railroad bridge crossing the Arkansas River since it is the closest to the point where the Arkansas flows into the Mississippi. Today this swampy delta area is known for an abundance of birds and snakes, both of which were equally prevalent in 1949.

Tuesday, July 26

Not much to tell about today. We pushed hard to get to Yancopin. Finally got to the bridge and since John wasn't feeling good Dick and Jerry walked into town. It was necessary to walk for a half mile on the bridge (RR). Coming back from town we were caught in the middle of the bridge by a handcar. Ran to the other side. Were entirely exhausted. Made camp early.

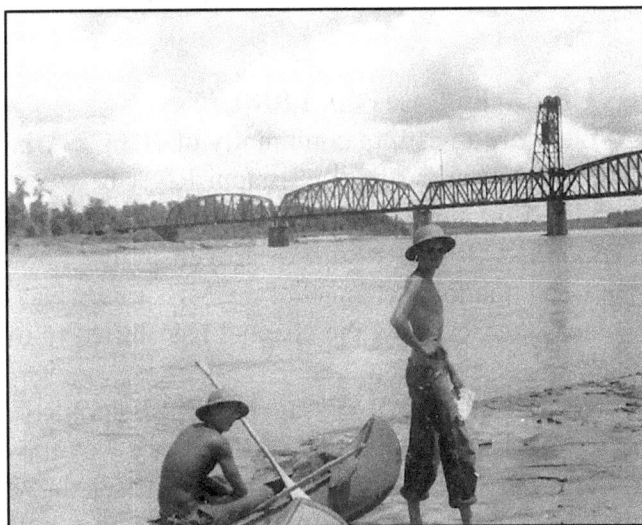

Johnny and Jerry discuss their plans with the Yancopin Rail-
bridge in the background. It's hard to imagine running from a
train, even a train handcar, on such a long, high bridge.

It's not surprising they made camp early after running from the train handcar. It's unclear what town they walked to, since Yancopin is not listed as a town. It may have been Watson, which is four or five miles south of the river.

Watson, Arkansas (Pop. 309)

When Watson was first settled, its position in the Arkansas Delta near the Mississippi was ideal for trade and traffic. French trappers and native Quapaw camped there and used the Red Fork Bayou as a shortcut to the Mississippi when the water was high enough. By the turn of the century, Watson had eight churches and seven saloons. Though inundated and nearly destroyed by the flood of 1927, Watson managed to recover and was a small, but thriving farm community into the 1950's. Mechanization of farms has reduced the need for farm labor, and the city population has declined since then.

Arkansas City, Arkansas (Pop. 1,018)

At one time a bustling community of 10,000, Arkansas City was an important stop on the Mississippi River between St. Louis and Vicksburg. Like many small towns in the Arkansas River delta region, Arkansas City was nearly destroyed by the flood of 1927. Before the flood, the main channel of the Mississippi was right next to the business district. Now the channel has shifted to over a mile away.

The Arkansas River flows into the Mississippi River north of Arkansas City. It is hard to estimate the distance they traveled from the mouth of the Arkansas River to Arkansas City on the Mississippi River since both rivers have shifted considerably over the last 60 plus years. Johnny, Dick, and Jerry probably traveled somewhere between 25 and 30 miles on the water, depending which way they went around some of the islands along the way. One of these islands, Choctaw Bar Island, makes up 200 square acres of the Choctaw Island Wildlife Management Area, well known for hunting, fishing, and birding.

Wednesday, July 27

 45 days since leaving Denver and we came into the Mississippi River today. At long last. After 2000 miles of travel. We were disappointed with the river. It's not as bad as we have heard. One thing that will give us trouble is the large boats. 3 of them passed us today. Got to Arkansas City and got water there and some food. Had to fix food over open fire no gas. Camped on Miss. River.

Dick Henke is ready for the river ahead. A video taken during the trip shows Dick or Johnny holding a bottle of beer in one hand and his pistol in the other. He shoots the top off and takes a good swig from the bottle.

On the Mighty Mississippi

July 27 to August 17
Greenville, Mississippi to New Orleans, Louisiana

In some ways, the Mississippi River was actually easier to canoe. There was less debris in the river, and the currents were not as tricky, but high water and huge wakes from large watercraft did cause difficulty.

While the Mississippi was calmer water than the Arkansas, the heat was nearly unbearable and the sun on the water made the glare blinding. Although afternoon downpours cooled them off briefly, the rain left them wet and steamy, adding to their discomfort. They found they could travel only six hours a day, avoiding the hottest part of the afternoon whenever possible. Due to the slower current, they could average only three miles per hour on the Mississippi, whereas they had made an average of six to eight miles per hour on the Arkansas. All these factors put them behind schedule for reaching New Orleans. Once on the Mississippi River, the young men made up time by getting a tow now and again from barges.

Greenville, Mississippi (Pop. 29,936)

Greenville sits east of the Mississippi River on the highest ground between Memphis and Vicksburg, next to Lake Ferguson, an oxbow lake leftover from an earlier river channel. A levee built in the 1930's straightened a bend in the Mississippi forming the lake. As the Mississippi sweeps past, Lake Ferguson curls off northward like a tendril. The mouth of the lake is protected by a peninsula jutting into the Mississippi. The lake provides a prime slackwater harbor for Greenville.

Long before Choctaw, Chickasaw, or Europeans lived in the area, indigenous people built the Winterville Mounds north of the city. The city of Greenville was founded in 1824. In 1863, Union troops utterly destroyed the city. As an important port on the Mississippi River, Greenville was rebuilt in 1865. The city was nearly destroyed again in the devastating flood of 1927, when the levee broke, and 10 feet of water buried the town and surrounding area for three months. Greenville cleaned up once more, and by the 1940's this vital port city was famous for blues clubs.

With a span of 840 feet, Benjamin G. Humphrey Bridge built in 1940 between Greenville, MS and Lake Village AR, was the longest vehicle bridge crossing the Mississippi until 1943, but the bridge's location just downriver from a sharp bend made it prone to barge collisions. The bridge was replaced in 2010. (Photo by John Weeks)

Thursday, July 28

Up at 9 AM cooked Pancakes for breakfast and ran out of fuel for stove. Saw a sand barge loading up so went over and talked to the captain. He offered to tow us to Greenville, Miss. So naturally we accepted. He told us many things about the river including signals used on the river. He towed us 35 miles into Greenville, Miss. and we cleaned up and went into town. Ate dinner and did some shopping. Were on another Radio interview. We were also taken through the local Yacht club for a show. Called home and slept on the beach by the boats.

Friday, July 29

Up at 5:30 and talked with some men that were doing some work on a tug boat. Then to a breakfast of pancakes at a local lunch counter. Picked up white gas at the Rose Service Station and walked back to the boats. Saw a tug boat so went over and talked to the captain. YEP we GOT a RIDE out of the dead water of the harbor to the river then he went to Memphis and we toward N.O. La. Passed by a stern wheeler today and also a very bad whirl pool near a bridge. We decided to arrive in Vicksburg Monday instead of Saturday so camped on a sand bar again. Ate 4 cans [lg.] of Pork and Beans and 6 cups hot chocolate. Swam in the river and went to bed.

Tugs, sternwheelers, barges and other large boats posed problems for the canoeists on the Mississippi River. This towboat, the Herbert Hoover, with six barges is similar to the tug boat that gave Johnny, Dick, and Jerry a tow. (Photo taken in 1938, near St. Louis, by U.S. Dept. of Defense. National Archives.)

Lake Providence, Louisiana (Pop. 4,123)

European settlers came to the Lake Providence area after the 1830 Indian Removal Act. They cleared cypress swamps and set up large cotton plantations. River transportation, especially steamboats, proved invaluable for shipping the cotton, but also provided ample opportunities for pirates to attack. A river bend near Lake Providence called Bunch's Bend was notorious as a place for pirates to kill the longboat men and steal their products. Anyone passing the bend without being killed or robbed was said to have made it to Providence.

The actual city of Lake Providence began as a supply depot for Union troops in 1862, and soon became a refugee camp for freed or runaway slaves, who were called contraband at the time. During the war years and immediately after, scalawags leased many of the abandoned plantations and hired African-American workers. However, due to minimal oversight or legal enforcement of the new laws, many abuses occurred and these Black workers were often paid little or nothing. In spite of new federal laws guaranteeing the right to vote, Louisiana passed voter registration laws that effectively prevented Blacks from voting until 1962, even though the area was, and still is, predominately African-American.

Saturday, July 30

We finally got into Louisiana today.[1] We stopped for a while in Lake Providence. We talked to a Negro fisherman who showed us a 75 pound fish - really big. We still find it difficult to travel during the middle of the day. The Negro was 62 years old and was in better physical condition that we. Traveled till 6:00 and then made camp. Had not seen one boat all day, but the minute we camped, the boats started coming by.

---

[1]   Note the Mississippi River forms the border between Louisiana and Mississippi at this point. The canoeists stopped on whichever side of the river offered the most convenient camping or had the city they hoped to visit.

Sunday, July 31

Got up this morning for the first time in a long time at 5:00, broke camp at 6:30 and traveled till 10:30. Saw the outskirts of Vicksburg so stopped. No sooner than it started to rain. Rained all afternoon so we slept. Saw the biggest boat we have ever seen. It was the engineers[2] moving. Will get to Vicksburg tomorrow.

Vicksburg, Mississippi (Pop. 27,948)

Vicksburg is probably best known for the 47 day siege of the city by Union forces during the Civil War, and its surrender in 1863. This devastating defeat haunted Vicksburg's residents so much they did not celebrate Independence Day until 1945. But the struggle for control of Vicksburg began much earlier. The French built a fort in 1719, but were massacred by the native Natchez. The Choctaw settled in the area after they helped defeat the Natchez. The Spanish built a fort called Fort Nogales in 1790. The Americans took control in 1798, calling the place Walnut Hills. (Nogales means walnut trees.) The Indian Removal Act began the removal of the Choctaw in 1801. The city now known as Vicksburg was founded in 1811, and incorporated in 1825.

One reason Vicksburg has been so important to so many people is its position high on the bluffs at the confluence of the Mississippi River and the Yazoo River. A sharp bend, called a meander, in the Mississippi River gives Vicksburg a commanding view of all river traffic. Called the "Key to the South," Vicksburg has the only railroad bridge between Baton Rouge and Memphis, and the only highway crossing between Natchez and Greenville. Vicksburg was prominent in the days of steamboat traffic, and remains a vibrant port city today.

In the following diary entry, Johnny says they tied up at the *Sprague*. The *Sprague* was the largest steam powered stern wheel tow boat ever built: 318 feet long with a wheel having a diameter of

---

[2]   This probably refers to the U.S. Army Corps of Engineers, who were responsible for dredging the river.

Although the Sprague no longer graces the Vicksburg water front, a beautiful mural commemorates the magnificent tug. This photo of the mural was taken in 2010 by Heironymous Rowe.

38 feet. Launched in 1901 and restructured in 1903, the *Sprague* set a record in 1907 for the largest tow completed. In the great Mississippi River flood of 1927, the *Sprague* carried 20,000 refugees from the flooded city of Greenville to the tent city set up by the Red Cross in Vicksburg. The *Sprague* was decommissioned in 1948 after having traveled some 996,000 miles. She ended up in Vicksburg's Riverside Park shortly thereafter, where she was used as a theatre and river museum for many years. Unfortunately, fire destroyed most of the structure in 1974. Johnny, Dick, and Jerry's two canoes seemed awfully small alongside the massive tug.

Monday, August 1

Got up late and got into Vicksburg around 11:00. Tied up on the Sprague and then went to news office. Then to P.O. and to the C of C[3]. Got material to find out where everything in town was at. Got a room in private home and then went to 2 shows. Went back to room and landlady called newspaper! We had an interview, then to bed.

---

[3]   Chamber of Commerce

Dick wrote home from Vicksburg.

Aug 1, 1949
Hi Mom, Dad & Bob,
　　　Thanks for the cash included in the envelope
but it really wasn't necessary. We hope to be in New
Orleans in 10 days or less. Did you know that the
Mayor of Little Rock Ark gave us a letter of introduction
to the Mayor of New Orleans? Travel on the
Mississippi River isn't so bad as we had expected.
The current is good so far and snags & sawyers few.
The only trouble is when steam boats pass us going
downstream. They kick up waves 3 or 4 ft high and we
have quite a time to keep from getting swamped. Bugs
& Mosquitoes are getting worse but it won't be long
till we're there. Will be glad to help work on the cabin
when we get home. Weather so hot & wet now we
can't travel more than about 6 hrs. a day without
burning to a crisp (good sun tan). We landed in
Vicksburg Miss. today and tied up to the Sprague,
the largest stern wheeler ever built. It's a gated
club now and was de-commissioned last year. From
stories we've heard about it people used to shoot at it
with hi—powered rifles when it went by because it
kicked up so much of a wake it washed the house boats
out of the river. Write New Orleans next and I'll see
you soon.
　　　　　Love,
　　　　　　　Dick
P.S. Any clippings I send to you keep them.
　　　John & Jerry have duplicates.

In Vicksburg, they stayed with Mr. and Mrs. Reddoch on
1005 Locust St. Built in 1900, this beautiful home with a wide
front porch and tapered square columns supporting an overhanging
balcony is now listed as part of the Vicksburg Historic District. In

95

Vicksburg, Johnny, Dick, and Jerry planned to see the Waterways Experiment Station featuring a model of the Mississippi. This 673 acre complex was the first federal hydraulic research station. It was built in response to the devastating 1927 flood. Operated by the U. S. Army Corps of Engineers, WES conducts key research in many different areas of science and engineering, including hydraulics, coastal engineering, flood control, and geotechnical engineering. Although they didn't get to see everything they had wanted to, Johnny enjoyed Vicksburg, and playfully wrote the following letter home.

Aug. 2 Vicksburg Miss
From The honorable J. M. Evert Jr. to New Orleans Canoe Expedition. Miss River in 45 days New Long Distance record on the Ark. River. General Deliv. New Orleans

Dearest Berniece,

Yes, honey it is hot here; so hot that I never want to return but it's worth it now at least. Sorry I couldn't write sooner but either I couldn't get time or something else prevented it. That's too bad about there being trouble between Mel and Shirley but I hope everything works out alright. Of course I am going. (If they let me) and so are you, I hope. Thanks for the kind offer of money but don't send it yet. As far as kidding goes, I never kid about either you, my love for you or my love for money. I can hardly wait to get back to see you and hold you and maybe try to say a little of what I feel in my heart. My only hope is that you love me a little but if you don't I love enough for two.

How about those pictures you were going to send? And by the way, say hello to Arlene and the rest of the gang. If you think this is bad try to read the other side.

Three pages of Johnny's letter, reproduced here, (below and pages 99, 101) show Johnny's creative whimsy. Writing sideways, then in a circular pattern, and then every other word upside down, Johnny was already anticipating meeting Berniece back in Denver.

As you probably already know, we had a wonderful reception in Little Rock and Ozark also Pine Bluff and Ft. Smith. In Ft. Smith we had a steak dinner, several radio Broadcasts, newspapers, police and boy escort and food from one of the groceries. At Ozark, we were met by the Mayor and almost all the local bums and beer drinkers. It seems we attract more dogs, small children, old men and bums than even a circus or a big fire. In Little Rock we were greeted by the Mayor, Broadcasts, free rooms, a big box of free food, beer and cigarettes. Left there after a wonderful time and went to Pine Bluff where we were entertained by the Chamber of Commerce at a dance (only one, and with a big ugly singer) and a steak dinner, also all the beer we could drink. We drank a lot. Before the steak dinner Jerry and I ate five (5) hamburgers, three glasses of milk and pie. As usual we were still hungry. Dick and Jerry have fine beards now but I have the blackest tan. We go into the colored entrance in shows now since we are all pretty dark. By the way, they have some very beautiful dark girls down here that have looked at me more than once but don't worry.

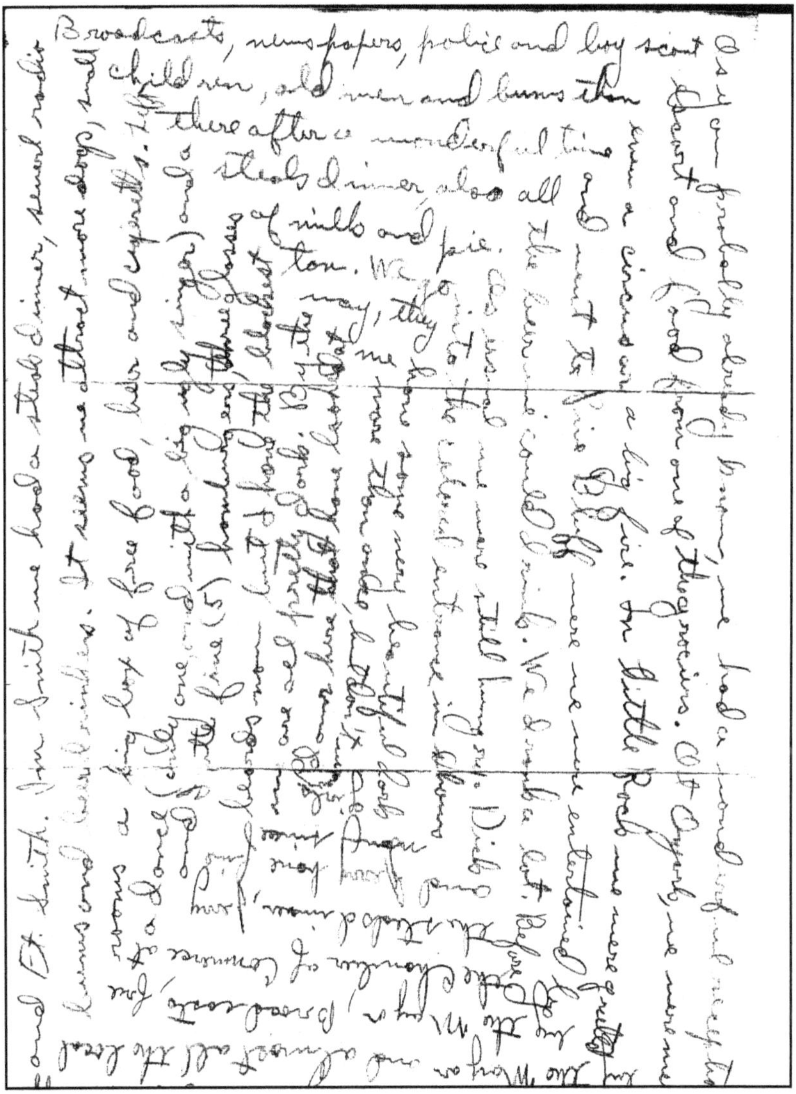

Broadcasts, newspapers, police and boy scout

children, old men and bums then

there after a wonderful time

all the

steak, dinner also

milk and pie

ton. We

It was really a thrill to see the good old Mississippi after working for it so hard, But it isn't all it is cracked up to be. (Too much strain writing that way so you get off easy)[4]

Stopped at Greenville, Miss. and it's a nice town but too hot and too much racial prejudice there. We got a ride on a tug boat from Ark. City, Ark to Greenville and from Greenville part way to Vicksburg. Got into Vicksburg Monday morning but didn't get to see any of the historical spots. As you know, this was a very important town during the Civil War. After months of planning, fighting and attacking, Grant finally took the town. The town surrendered on July 4th, 1863 and from then on Vicksburg never celebrated July 4th. They finally gave in in the year 1945 and it made national headlines that Vicksburg finally lost the war.

We are going to try to get to New Orleans by the 12th but I don't know if we can make it. That's a long, hard pull in this heat.

I can hardly wait to get back to skiing again. That about all we can talk or think about anymore. This year, you are going up more often if I have anything to say about it. I might even try ice-skating but just for you and not because I like it. Please keep up the swell letters and save a little love for the guy who loves you most of all. -I'll see you in my dreams--

Write to Baton Rouge or New Orleans and start looking for an apartment for me. Thanks honey,
Love, Johnny.

---

[4]   On page 3 Johnny started by writing one word right side up and the next upside down, but he gave up after just a few sentences. Note: page 4 was written normally, and is not reproduced here.

really a thrill I see... good Mississippi... working... it... it isn't... it... checked... to be.
(Too much strain working that way so you get off easy.)

Stopped at Greenville, Miss. and its' a nice town but too hot and too much racial prejudice there. We got a ride on a tug but from Ark. City, Ark. to Greenville and from Greenville part way to Vicksburg. Got into Vicksburg Monday morning but didn't get to see any of the historical spots. As you know, this was a very important town during the Civil War. After months of planning, fighting and attacking, Grant finally took the town. The town surrendered on July 4th 1863 and from then on Vicksburg never celebrated July 4th. They finally gave in in the year 1945 and it made national headlines that Vicksburg finally lost the War.

We are going to try to get to

Tuesday, August 2

Got up and ate and went to P.O. No mail. Went to boats and got water and food. We shoved off at 11:30 and paddled till 2:00 then we decided to loaf, so as to get in Natchez on Thursday. Made camp on a small island which seemed to be slowly disappearing.

Fortunately, the island did not disappear overnight.

Wednesday, August 3

Island isn't smaller, in fact much larger. Decided to rest today since it is only a short way to Natchez. We found a good swimming spot off the island and spent most of the day swimming. Also listened to the radio. It's still working good. Took some pictures. Got to bed early since we were getting up early.

Natchez, Mississippi (Pop. 22,740)

Natchez is a beautiful Southern city, on the east bank of the Mississippi River. Scores of antebellum houses and live oak trees line the city streets. Seated on the highest bluff north of the Gulf of Mexico, Natchez is the oldest European settlement on the Mississippi River, starting with French settlers who built Fort Rosalie there in 1716. The Natchez Indians killed 229 French colonists in 1729, and the French killed most of the Natchez in response. At various times, British or Spanish forces ruled the area until the Americans took it in 1783. Natchez became the capital of Mississippi Territory in 1798. In 1817, Natchez became the first capital of the state of Mississippi, only to be replaced by Jackson in 1822.

Natchez was the terminus of the famous Natchez Trace. For years keelboats and barges coming down the river sold their goods and the lumber from the ship in Natchez, then walked back to Nashville, Tennessee. The trip back took three to four weeks over rough ground. In 1742, French travelers described the trail as "miserable." Later, Thomas Jefferson ordered the 450 mile forest road to be widened in order to tie the Mississippi River and the new Louisiana Purchase to the rest of the country. The resulting Natchez Trace, no more than 12 feet wide in places, was the most traveled road in the southwest before 1817.

The lower part of the city, called Natchez Under-the-Hill, became notorious for violence and lawlessness. Travelers unlucky enough to stop at a 'trapdoor' saloon might be beaten, robbed and dumped into the Mississippi River through a trapdoor in the floor. Steamboats played an important role in the development of Natchez also. The first steamboat coming down river in 1811 had a wild ride, surviving the first of the three major New Madrid earthquakes in 1811-1812. These earthquakes and their many aftershocks were the largest earthquakes east of the Rockies ever recorded in America, with estimated magnitudes ranging from 7.5 to 7.7. The quakes caused landslides, sand blows, and sinks. Islands disappeared and the Mississippi ran backwards for a while. Native Americans on shore blamed the steamboat chugging down river and belching black smoke for the quake and tried to attack it. They paddled their canoes almost as fast as the steamboat could travel, but couldn't keep it up indefinitely and eventually gave up the chase. This same steamboat picked up a load of cotton in Natchez, the first of thousands such bales shipped to New Orleans by steamboat over the next decades.

Currently two bridges span the Mississippi River at Natchez, but in 1949 there was only one bridge, built in 1940.

Thursday, August 4

Again our calculations were wrong. It took us seven hours to get to Natchez. Went to show and then to News. They had been waiting and hunting for us all day. Got our food and left town in the dark. Got five miles down stream and put the tent up and went to bed.

Both the Arkansas and the Mississippi Rivers are extremely sinuous, with uncharted backwaters, meanders, and shifting sandbar islands, making it hard to guess times and distances. As the Mississippi curls back and forth across the broad valley, the river route is much longer than driving would be.

Friday, August 5
　　Made a very early start and traveled for 4 hrs. then stopped. Figuring on traveling four hours at night eve. Mid way thru our lunch it started to rain. Sat in rain and got all wet. Then put up tent to dry off and warm up. Started again at 6 and traveled until 9:00 then made a dark camp. Tired from night travel. Made 43 miles. Dick in swamp- lizard mos. spider pictures.

Unfortunately, the pictures Dick took of lizards, mosquitos and spiders in the swamp have not survived.

Saturday, August 6
　　Tired from night before but started moving at 6. Traveled till noon got caught in the rain so stopped and swam during the rain. Then started ahead again till 6 Went to bed. Sand bars scarce— mostly mud. Low on food, water.

With all the rain, it became harder and harder to find a decent place to camp each night. Jerry told about one camp they started to set up on a marshy bank. Johnny went into the reeds to take care of business, but soon came flying back out and dove into the river. The horseflies were practically eating him alive! The trio struck what little camp they had made, and went on until they found a sandbar where the flies were not so bad.

Finding places to stop and restock their food and water was also difficult in this part of the river. Of course, they had fishing gear along, but they never could catch any fish to cook. Johnny was much more used to 'fishing' with blasting caps than with a hook and a line.

Sunday, August 7
　　Got up at 6 AM traveled 4 hr. and found a good camp site and settled down cleaning things up for the rest of the day.

Baton Rouge, Louisiana (Pop. 125,629)

Baton Rouge, the second largest city and the capital of Louisiana, is in the southeast part of the state on the first Mississippi River bluffs upriver from the delta. It is the northernmost port on the Mississippi River able to accommodate Panamax ships, which are the size of ship that can pass through the Panama Canal.

The name of the city is French for "red stick," stemming from a red cypress pole hung with bloody animals that marked the boundary between the Houma and the Goula tribes in 1699 when Sieur D'Iberville's exploration party came upon the place. Archeological evidence shows the area has been inhabited since 8,000 B.C. In 1719, the French built a post there. Since then, Baton Rouge has been governed by France, Britain, Spain, Louisiana, the Florida Republic, the Confederate States, and the United States. This rich

The State Capitol, which houses the governor's office, was completed in 1932. The project was pushed forward by Louisiana Governor Huey Long, who was later assassinated in the building. Huey Long was the brother of Earl Long, Louisiana's governor in 1949. (Photo by Richard Rutter)

cultural heritage was also enhanced by the French-Canadians, who were expelled from Acadia, Canada in 1755. The groups settling in the Louisiana region became known as Cajuns, a word formed from an alteration of the French pronunciation for Acadia.

Baton Rouge was incorporated in 1817, and became the state capital in 1849. Occupied by Union troops in 1862, Baton Rouge was reinstated as the seat of Louisiana government in 1882.

Monday, August 8
Up at 6. Left at 7:00. Went till 9:00. Rested till 10:00. Went on to Baton Rouge and we met Chamber of Commerce changed clothes and went to the Governor. Had coffee with the Governor's asst. and were escorted around town. Saw University of La. Very nice architecture. following mode of Construction as to subject taught there.[5] Slept on barge in Miss. Not much sleep.

All along, reaching Baton Rouge, the capital of Louisiana, had been a major goal since they were carrying a letter of introduction from Governor William Knous of Colorado to Governor Earl Long of Louisiana. The letter, sealed and wrapped in black oilcloth had survived rainstorms, capsizing, and theft. Now the adventurers were anxious to deliver it. The diary says they changed clothes, but by this point they had spent nearly two months on the river. Johnny described the trio as scruffy. They wore faded blue jeans and white t-shirts with sleeves rolled up. Deeply tanned, strong from days of paddling, each with a long knife strapped to one leg, they rivaled the mountain men and river scouts first exploring the west.

At the governor's office, they were served cookies and tiny sandwiches with the crusts cut off. The coffee, a special blend with

---

[5]   The main branch of Louisiana State University is in Baton Rouge and boasts architecture designed in the Italian Renaissance Style. The diary entry above refers to the academic buildings forming the quad, modeled after Thomas Jefferson's University of Virginia Campus. Each of the buildings represents a different discipline.

In spite of cleaning up for the governor, (below) Johnny, Jerry, and Dick felt underdressed for the occasion. The photo to the left shows Jerry wearing one of the long knives each carried.

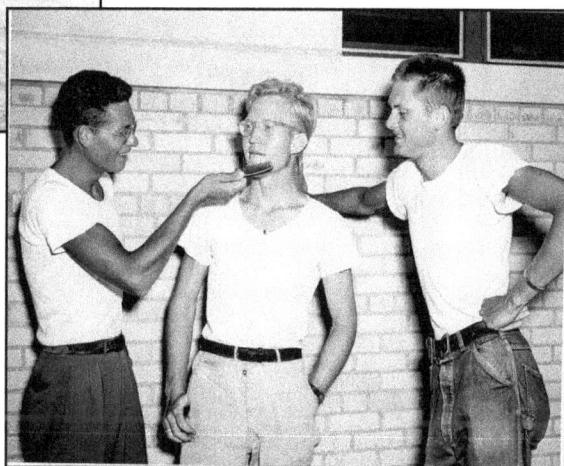

chicory, was served in cups so thin and delicate that Johnny was afraid they would break. The coffee was delicious, and the atmosphere genteel, but they enjoyed it with Senator A. A. Fredericks, the executive secretary to the Governor. Governor Long was not there. He was hunting in Colorado with his friend, Governor Knous.

A copy of the governor's letter is reproduced on the next page.

THE STATE OF COLORADO
EXECUTIVE CHAMBERS
DENVER

WILLIAM LEE KNOUS
GOVERNOR

May 27, 1949

Honorable Earl K. Long, Governor
State of Louisiana
Baton Rouge, Louisiana

Dear Governor Long:

This will introduce Dick Henke of Denver, Colorado who with his two companions, John Everet, Jr., and Jerry Pankow, also of Denver, are making a trip by water from Pueblo, Colorado to New Orleans, Louisiana.

Mr. Henke is an airlines major at the University of Denver and Mr. Pankow is a student in chemistry at the same university. All three are veterans of World War II.

They are conveying my greetings, as Governor of Colorado, to the State of Louisiana, by means of this unusual journey, and while, it is mainly the spirit of adventure which has prompted them to attempt this trip, the wholesome experiences so gained, will be of value to them.

Any courtesies extended to them will be greatly appreciated.

Sincerely,

Lee Knous,
Governor

LK/mlc

Dick and Johnny both wrote home from Baton Rouge.

Dear Mom & Dad   (also Bob)
    It was sure good to talk to you again and thanks for the "Buck" inserts in the letter. I really appreciate it. We see the Governors assistant again Friday and will be escorted through the capitol of the state (By the way, we had coffee with him yesterday.) Dad, I'll have to see what the score is in New Orleans but I'll try to get home and help on the cabin as soon as possible.
                    Love, Dick

Baton Rouge
Dearest,
    Well it won't be long now. We finally got to Baton Rouge and delivered the letter but not to the Gov. He wasn't in. Sen. Friedricks [sic] (Dem)[6] was very nice, and served us French coffee in the Governor's office. Very interesting. Sorry I don't get a chance to write more often and in letters instead of postcards but you know how it is. I should get back there by the 1st but in case I am not, don't celebrate, I will come back. The food down here is really different, but I still like the way you fix bacon and eggs. How about a date on the 2nd? Then the 3 day outing.[7] I am really looking forward to that. We are pretty broke but we can make it I think. Then we will have to work for awhile to get home. Think you would want a bum like me on your hands?
                    Love,   Johnny

---

[6]   Albert Asa Fredericks served four terms in the Louisiana State Senate. He served on the State Board of Education in addition to his role as the governor's executive secretary.
[7]   See page 59 for an explanation of the 3 day outing.

Hi Bob,

Well finally we are almost there! (Thank Goodness!) I'll match you for who has the best sun tan now. I hear you were up at 3 Island[8] and caught 20 trout. Lucky dog. We are 128[9] miles from New Orleans now and hope to get there Fri. Write me a postcard at New Orleans.

As Ever,   Dick

After the gracious reception in Baton Rouge, traveling on seemed anti-climactic. They were tired, both physically from weeks of hard paddling, and mentally from the trip itself. With more man-made levees, the scenery became monotonous. Mark Twain once described the Mississippi River below St. Louis as the least interesting part of the whole waterway, where the only things to watch were "the low shores, the ungainly trees and the democratic buzzards."[10] Before leaving Baton Rouge, in a moment reflecting their temporary discouragement, Johnny said, "You can give this canoeing back to the Indians. We set out looking for glamour but all we've seen are river banks and levees."[11]

While the scenery was less interesting, the river traffic caused more problems. High, flood-stage waters along with increasing barge traffic meant they had to be constantly vigilant to avoid being swamped. The three young men were also broke in spite of occasional care packages from home, and they worried about the time it would take to travel on down to New Orleans. September

---

[8]   Three Island Lake is almost 20 miles north of Steamboat Springs, Colorado, in the Routt National Forest. A popular fishing spot, the lake has a variety of fish including rainbow trout, bluegill, smallmouth bass and largemouth bass

[9]   From Baton Rouge to New Orleans is only 80.4 miles by road, but easily 128 miles by curling river.

[10]   - interview in *Chicago Tribune*, July 9, 1886

[11]   -interview in *Denver Post*, August. 10, 1949

was the deadline for their return to Denver, but they had no clear plan of how they would return. Wider and deeper than the Arkansas River, the Mississippi was also much slower; too slow in fact to allow them to finish the trip in the two months they had allowed. Their solution was to hook up with a tug or barge, and get a tow by working on deck.

Tuesday, August 9

Up at 5:00 with little or no sleep. Ate at restaurant and at 10:00 went to capitol again. Were escorted around and met 2 fellow canoeists whose boat sunk at Natchez and they were hitch hiking on to N.O. Joined forces and were to continue 5 of us in 2 boats to N.O. Slept on barge.

Tug moved barge at 1:30 in morning so we moved too and took our boats along with us. Up at 5:30 and at breakfast fixed pancakes, oranges, bread, etc. talked to captain of the Bob Francis and he said he'd tow us to N.O. We accepted.

—Photo by The Times-Picayune.
READING MAIL AFTER COMPLETING TRIP DOWN RIVER
From left: Pankow, Henke, Evert, Angell and Asker.

The three canoeists from Denver briefly joined forces with two canoeists from Dartmouth. The Dartmouth men started in Illinois, but sunk their canoe at Natchez. (Photo by permission of the *Times Picayune*, New Orleans, August 12, 1949.)

111

The Bob Francis was a big, ocean going tug, licensed to go up the Mississippi River as far as St. Louis, Missouri and to ply the intercoastal canal to Houston, Texas. This was a difficult license to procure and meant the captain really knew what he was doing; most tugs had a license to go only as far as Cairo, Illinois. All five travelers headed south on the tug, with the agreement to work for the ride. The captain started them off polishing brass. Jerry said they polished brass lamps, railings and turnbuckles. Riding the tug gave the travelers a chance to learn more about another kind of river work. Jerry still remembers he was offered a chance to act as helmsman. and enjoyed steering a craft that big.

Wednesday, August 10

Boarded ship at noon and loaded canoes in fair time. Left Baton Rouge at 3:00 and started to polish the Brass searchlights but got rained out. Ate in galley with crew. Really swell people on this ship. Did dishes for the cook. Expect to arrive in N.O. 2 or 3 in morning only $2.50 left between the 3 of us. Don't know what we'll do when we land.

Carville, Louisiana (Pop. unavailable)

Carville is approximately sixteen miles south of Baton Rouge. Currently it is listed as a neighborhood of St. Gabriel, but in 1949 it was the site of a Leper Hospital established in the 1890's. The facility was designed as a place of refuge for leprosy victims and their families. As such, Carville was not usually a place for steamboats, barges or tugs to stop, but that night the Bob Francis had engine trouble and they had to pull into the bank near Carville. Johnny had to jump from the bow to the river bank with a rope to tie off on some trees. The diesel engine had burned out a bearing. Replacing it was hard work and fairly tricky. They had to dismantle the cylinder, take out and replace the bearing and then put the cylinder back together, all in the dark. It took several hours to complete the repair. All in all, the work they did on the tug in exchange for a ride turned out to be harder and more exciting than they expected.

THURSDAY, AUGUST 11
ARRIVED NEW ORLEANS AT 5:07 AM
     Stayed up till 11:00 (Dick) and went to bed for about 2
hours on deck of tug boat. John & Jerry didn't get to bed at all.
They got ready to go to sleep and the diesel engine on the tug
burned out and a cam rod bearing. So John & Jerry got in with
the crew and started to help work on the engine and Dick bal-
anced alone on a ladder to tie the tug up till it could be repaired.
arrived in N.O. 5:07 in morning. No sleep.

Still no sleep for J & J. Cooked breakfast aboard ship and packed
equipment. Also carried canoes out of H2O. J went into newspaper got write-up and AP got story. Out to boats again, finished packing. Room at YMCA swim walked to Canal St. and
wandered through French Quarter very interesting indeed
Found Absinthe house and had a mint julep WOW $1.25 EA.[12]
WOW! AGAIN! WOT Hoppen? Ate at a small restaurant steak
and mashed spuds something fried very good.

     The breakfast they shared with the crew was delicious. Sixty
years later, Johnny still remembered the grits and sweet potato pie.
One of the crew shared the recipe for the pie, but Johnny said nothing was ever as good as the one he had that morning.
     Canal Street ends at the Mississippi River. This famous thor-
oughfare marks the upriver boundary of the French Quarter, called
the Vieux Carré. Canal Street divides the older Spanish/French colonial neighborhoods from the newer American sections.

----

[12]   Although they don't say so in the diary, they must have received
some money from home when they arrived in New Orleans. In an era
when a cup of coffee cost a dime and a beer might be 15 cents, the price
of the drink shocked them. A Mint Julep is made from bourbon, mint,
sugar and water. The bourbon was much stronger than what they were
used to.

Dick, Jerry, and Johnny found the Old Absinthe House on their first day in New Orleans. The Old Absinthe House is on the corner of Rue Bourbon and Rue Bienville in the French Quarter. It opened in 1807 as an import shop, but became famous in 1874 for serving absinthe. This traditionally green mixture is distilled from anise, wormwood, and other herbs to make a potent beverage (55% or 110 proof). Although it is not actually more dangerous than other spirits, many people thought absinthe was extremely addictive. Absinthe was banned in the United States by 1915. That ban was lifted in 2007.

Jerry and Johnny sit at the famous copper topped wooden bar inside the Old Absinthe House. The three canoeists had mint juleps here, a famous southern drink made from bourbon, sugar, water and mint. The drink was both more expensive and stronger than they expected.

New Orleans, Louisiana (Pop. 570,445)

More than anywhere else in the United States, New Orleans shows evidence of the cultural mélange that forms the nation. Native Americans, Africans (both free and slave), Spanish, French, and a host of others have helped shape New Orleans as one of the most important cities in the South.

In the 1690's the French built Port Bayou St. John at the head of the bayou linking Lake Pontchartrain to the Mississippi River. In 1701 they built Fort St. Jean at the mouth of the bayou. The city itself was founded in 1718 on an area of relatively high ground along the trade route the French established between forts. The city grew, but also attracted a population of wild and lawless men, including trappers, gold hunters and riffraff. In 1721, Pierre Charlevoix was not impressed, describing Nouvelle Orleans, as it is called it French, as having "several hundred wretched hovels in a malarious wet thicket of willows and dwarf palmettos, infested by serpents and alligators"[13] In spite of his negative comments, Charlevoix was convinced New Orleans would become important.

---

[13]   Charlevoix, Pierre. *History and General Description of New France,* 1722. Translated from French by John G. Shea, 1868.

Charlevoix's prediction proved true even sooner than he expected. In 1722, New Orleans became the capital of French Louisiana, but in September a hurricane destroyed most of the city. After the widespread destruction, a grid pattern for building, still noticeable in many places, was enforced. Situated as it is near the mouth of the Mississippi, New Orleans became crucial to both Colonial France and Colonial England.

In 1763, Britain won the worldwide conflict known as the Seven Years War and took over Louisiana colony east of the Mississippi. Spain was awarded the territory west of the Mississippi to compensate for the loss of Florida. In spite of growing commerce and the sugar industry, Spanish rule was problematic for years, with two devastating fires destroying hundreds of buildings. The city was rebuilt of brick, but the Spanish gave it to the French secretly in 1800, and Napoleon sold it to the United States in 1803.

In 1947, the Fort Lauderdale hurricane hit New Orleans. Many of the suburbs were flooded, but the city proper escaped major flooding. Two years later in 1949, the city had mostly recovered.

New Orleans has always been a unique city with its diverse cultures blending to create something found nowhere else on earth. Known for its spicy food, vibrant music, the French quarter, and wild celebrations, New Orleans was, and still is, a destination worth reaching. Johnny, Dick, and Jerry arrived in the city in a different way than most visitors, but they found that New Orleans was well worth the trip.

Friday, August 12

Up at 8:30 and met Jim and Dave went to meet the mayor DeLesseps Morrison and received the key to the city from him. Took off to be interviewed over a Radio program and on the program we received a pass & tickets to Pondchartrain [sic] Amusement Park. Spent afternoon in French quarter again. Saw Antoine Museum, Pirates Alley, Bourbon St. etc. Ate at a small French café and went out to Pondchartrain [sic] Beach. A lovely evening. Rode all the rides we wanted for free! To bed at 11:00

Friday was a day to relax and enjoy the sights. Antoine's is the most famous restaurant in New Orleans. Established in 1840 by Antoine Alciatore, it is the oldest family run restaurant in the city. The restaurant moved to its current, 'new' location in 1868. Antoine, a Frenchman who immigrated to New York and later moved to New Orleans, was dedicated to bringing a fine dining experience to the raucous town. He is famous for inventing Oysters Rockefeller, so named for their rich sauce. Antoine's has fourteen lavishly decorated dining rooms and is a museum in itself.

Pirate's Alley runs between St. Louis Basilica, the oldest active church in the United States, and Cabildo, which housed the government when the Louisiana Purchase was concluded. Paved with ballast stones from Mississippi River boats, the alley is named for Jean Lafitte, a locally popular smuggler/privateer/pirate. Legend has it that when Governor Claiborne put a price on his head, Lafitte put

Pontchartrain Beach and Amusement Park first opened in 1928 on the south shore of the lake, then moved in the early 1930's when the new levee altered the lake's shoreline. At its new location at the end of Elysian Fields Avenue, the beach and amusement park featured a roller coaster, ferris wheel, Zephyr, and many other rides. In 1949, Lake Pontchartrain beach was still segregated, for whites only. Pontchartrain Beach closed in 1983. (Postcard from Louisiana News Company, New Orleans, between 1930 and 1950.)

up handbills offering the same price for the arrest of the governor. Whether he was actually responsible for the handbills or not, the story shows Lafitte's popularity and audacity. Lafitte fought alongside Andrew Jackson in the 1814 Battle of New Orleans, against the British and in return received a pardon for his acts of smuggling.

Bourbon Street is in the heart of the French Quarter, stretching thirteen blocks from Canal Street to Esplanade Avenue. It was named for the French ruling family. Originally residential, Bourbon Street was known for its restaurants, bars, nightclubs, gambling houses, and brothels by the early 20th century.

Saturday, August 13

Went looking for a place to sell the boats. Cash running low ($3 for the 3 of us). Stopped at a Marine supply store and he said he'd bring the boats in for us and let us sell them from his store. So we did bring them in. Walked around town again all afternoon then came back to YMCA & swam, fenced, lifted weights, ran, etc. Very tired! Dick & Jerry walked over to Bourbon and Canal Sts. Walked for 1/2 an hour and came back. Too wild and wicked to suit us. To bed at 10:30.

Sunday, August 14

Up at 11:00 and breakfast. Wrapped up our swim suits and camera and went over to Pondchartrain [sic] Beach. Got a locker and spent till 6:00 o'clock swimming. Came back. Ate 2 sandwiches for dinner and went to see 3 Musketeers for 21¢[14] each. Called home after show for money.

Monday, August 15

As usual we got up late and decided to see if the boats had been sold. We went to Duvics and found to our gladness that the orange boat had been sold. We then decided to celebrate so got a beer. We went to show and then back to the Y and swam.

---

[14]   The average price of a movie in 1949 was about 45 cents.

A city park in New Orleans purchased the canoe to use in their growing rental program. In September, 1949, the New Orleans Recreation Department, (NORD) was celebrated in *Life* Magazine as one of the best such agencies in the United States. NORD built playground and pools, and developed a broad base of recreational activities from track races to opera and ballet. There were facilities for both Black and White children, but they were segregated.

Tuesday, August 15

Went again to find if the second boat had been sold. It had not. We were told to come back Wed. Went for a bread meal again. Have to conserve the money. Went on a tour of French Quarter. Saw everything we had seen before but got the history. Y and swimming again. Chess was also enjoyed.

Wednesday, August 16

Still no boat sold might have to sell at less. It's hard to make up our minds what to do. Will leave tomorrow no matter what. Went to show tonight and also did more swimming. Chess is the order of the day.

Although they had enjoyed the novelty of New Orleans, Johnny, Dick, and Jerry were ready to go home. None of their plans for obtaining motorcycles worked, and selling the boats proved more difficult than they imagined. Tired of the heat, out of money, and anxious to get back in time for the start of school and to help out on the cabin Dick's folks were building, they decided in the end to take a bus home, even though it meant selling the canoe at a loss and borrowing enough money for the ticket and meals during the two and a half day bus ride. Dick and Johnny both wrote from the YMCA about their final plans concerning how they would return to Denver.

Public Correspondence
Young Men's Christian Association
936 St. Charles Street
New Orleans 12, Louisiana

Dear Mom & Dad,
    We have finally decided to come home
by bus. We leave here (N.O.) at 7:30 PM TODAY
(Thurs) and arrive at Trailways depot at 11:15
late Monday.[15] We've had a swell stay in town but
it costs too much. Sold the orange boat for $50
and if a customer doesn't buy the blue one for
$100 we sell it to a dealer for $60 so we can
get home. Please have a big meal ready for
Sat evening and a tall! cool! glass of beer.
    You will recognize me by a mustache
and a short black beard. If everything goes
OK I expect to have a live alligator for Allen
but don't tell him that. If I get the thing for
him I don't eat so well on the way but it might
be worth it to see the expression on his face.
I guess that's all for now.
    We have an awful lot to do between
now and 7:30. See you Sat unless you are
at the cabin.
        Love,
           Dick

---

[15]   Dick says they will arrive Monday, while Johnny says it will be
Saturday. Since the picture of their arrival ran on Monday, Johnny was
likely correct.

Public Correspondence
Young Men's Christian Association
936 St. Charles Street
New Orleans 12, Louisiana

Dearest Berniece,

After almost giving up hope, I finally got
your letter. Now to answer your questions one
by one; we are coming back by bus and leaving
today (Thurs) and will get in Denver sometime
Saturday. We couldn't get a deal for the motorcycles
so we decided to hitch-hike, then cancelled that
idea in favor of the bus. We are really taking a
beating on the canoes, but we can't do much
about it. Very few jobs down here and the heat
is too oppressive for any but the colored to work.

The picture was swell but where did you
say it was taken? Would you call Terry, my brother,
and give him your phone number so I can call when
I get home-otherwise I don't know how to reach
you, O.K? Well honey, there's not much more to
tell you except that I love you very much.

You are the best thing that ever happened
to me but evidently you don't feel the same[16]
so I'll just say-

Love, Johnny

---

[16]   Berniece had not accepted or rejected Johnny at this point. She
was hesitating partly because other young men were courting her.

Thursday, August 17

Up at 9:00 and ate the usual. Then came back and checked out of the YMCA. Walked to Post Office and wrote home an airmail letter telling time of arrival. Went over to Duvics and checked to see if he had sold our boat. No luck. So we had to sell it to him for $60 instead of a $100. We had to borrow $10 each as a personal loan from Duvic to have enough to buy a couple of presents and eat on the way. I think we were stung but what could we do? Bought a live alligator for Allen Henke and a lot of other presents for all and boarded bus at New Orleans terminal at 7:30. OUR TRIP IS OVER! A SUCCESS!
The End

Johnny, Dick, and Jerry came home with beards and paddles, a four foot long baby alligator from the French Quarter, and nearly empty pockets. They were honorary citizens of Little Rock, and carried keys to the cities of Baton Rouge and New Orleans. Though never officially recorded, they believe they broke the long distance record for traveling the 1900 mile stretch of the Arkansas from Pueblo to its mouth even with the portage caused by the lack of water after the John Martin Dam. They had been celebrated and welcomed in small towns and big cities and had seen a chunk of America ranging from the wild west to the deep south; an America destined to change radically in the following decade.

Equally important is the friendship that developed between these young men. Throughout two months of demanding travel, the three remained good friends facing each new challenge as a team. Bad weather, stolen guns, broken ribs, sunburn, snags, and sawyers wore them out, but never drove them apart. Jerry said, "We were all three good friends and made the trip without any disagreement, which is remarkable considering we were our only company for most of the time. It was and 'is' a treasured period of my life."

On a deeper level, the trip was a healing journey for the young men. Johnny said the trip restored some of their faith in humanity. When they came back from the war, Dick said they had had

122

"a twisted view toward human beings and their reactions toward one another, but people along the river were mostly so friendly and cordial that we altered our view." Except for the salvage artist in Muskogee, they all three praised the kindness of the people they met, and claimed meeting so many wonderful people was a true highlight of the trip. More than anything else, Johnny, Dick, and Jerry came home with a renewed sense of what was right in the world and a lifetime of memories.

Paddled Own Canoe; Now Home Again

The adventurous trio of University of Denver students who took a 2,700-mile river trip from Pueblo, Colo., to New Orleans are back again. Above, the bearded boys, proudly carrying their oars, are shown receiving greetings. Shown (left to right) are: John Evert Jr., Mrs. John Evert, his mother; Jerry Pankow; his sister, Barbara; his mother, Mrs. E. G. Pankow; Mrs. R. C. Henke and her son, Dick Henke. The homefolks met them at the bus station.

Photo and article originally published on August 21, 1949 in *The Denver Post*.

Epilogue

The baby alligator Dick brought home lived for a short time in his basement. Dick fed it raw hamburger, but the alligator apparently pined for its old home in Louisiana. It escaped and crawled under the furnace. Resisting all entreaties and temptations to come out, the alligator died shortly thereafter.

After returning from the trip down the Arkansas, Jerry Pankow finished school at Denver University with a degree in chemistry, and some courses in anthropology and archeology. After graduating, he then headed for Texas. He had jobs in Texas and California before he moved back to Denver and through Dick went to work for Martin/Martin, a civil engineering company. He met Mollie, another Walther leaguer, and married her. They had three children, Jeff, Marcine, and Paul. He and Mollie were amateur archeologists for many years. In 2005, Jerry wrote a book about his work at the Claiborne site in Louisisana. Jerry currently lives in Slidell, Louisiana.

Dick also finished school at the University of Denver. He met and married Dee. They lived for awhile in Seattle, Washington, but eventually moved back to the Rockies where they built a cabin. They had four children, Wade, Wayne, Cindi and Cheri. Dick died in a dynamite accident while digging a well in the early 60's.

Johnny married the girl of his dreams, Berniece. They had six children, Brian, Terri Ann, Denise, Lisa, Mike and Chris. After a time in Seattle, San Francisco, and San Bruno, they settled in San Jose, California. After a stroke in the early 80's, Johnny bought a small cottage in Ireland and lived there until he died in April, 2012.

In 1952, three years after his river trip, Johnny bought a plane and got a pilot's license. He and Berniece, along with Dick and Dee, headed toward Alaska in a couple of small planes with the idea of becoming bush pilots. But that's another story.

RADIO COVERAGE

The canoeists participated in radio broadcasts from these stations.

KGHF	Pueblo, CO
KWBW	Hutchinson, KS
KSOK	Arkansas City, KS
KFPW	Fort Smith AR (multiple broadcasts, may have included other stations)
KTLN	(Denver Station, interviewed in Little Rock, AR)
KVLC	Little Rock, AR

They also made radio broadcasts in the following cities, but did not name the stations.

> Pine Bluff, AR
> Greenville. MS
> New Orleans, LA

In addition, radio broadcasts were made from other cities not named in either the diary or the letters. Some of these were re-broadcast in Denver. Mrs. Pankow, Jerry's mother, noted the following:

6/21:   2 pm   Denver station unknown, from Garden City, Kansas
6/27:   10 am KMYR Denver, broadcast location unknown
6/30:   7 am   KOA Denver, broadcast location unknown
7/1:   9 am   KMYR Denver, from Arkansas City, Arkansas
7/7:   9 am   KMYR Denver, from Tulsa, Oklahoma
8/10:   7:45 am KLZ Denver, from Baton Rouge, Louisiana
8/12:   9 am   KMYR Denver, from New Orleans, Louisiana
8/21:   8 pm   KMYR Denver, from Denver

NEWSPAPER COVERAGE

Many newspapers ran articles about the trip. Johnny, Dick and Jerry also wrote articles to send to various papers, including the *Arkansas Gazette* and the *Arkansas Valley Journal*. Articles and pictures from the following newspapers helped inform this manuscript.

Arkansas City Traveler, Arkansas City, Kansas
Arkansas Gazette, Little Rock, Arkansas
Associated Press (articles, photos in several papers)
The Commercial, Pine Bluff, Arkansas
Denver Post, Denver Colorado
Garden City Daily Telegram, Garden City, Kansas
The Hutchinson News, Hutchinson, Kansas
Lamar Ledger, Lamar, Colorado
Natchez Democrat, Natchez, Mississippi
Ponca City News, Ponca City, Oklahoma
Rocky Mountain News, Denver, Colorado
State-Times, Baton Rouge, Louisiana
The Times Picayune, New Orleans, Louisiana
Tribune Democrat, La Junta, Colorado
Vicksburg Post, Vicksburg, Mississippi
The Wichita Eagle, Wichita, Kansas
Tulsa World, Tulsa, Oklahoma

Glossary

bayou: pronounced by-yo in Natchez, by-you in the most of the
    rest of Louisiana and many other states
    in Natchez: a deep ravine, not necessarily with water.
    elsewhere: a slow-moving, shallow stream draining a swamp
    or marking an abandoned river channel.

deadwater: an area in a river or bay without current, or areas where
    brackish freshwater sits on top of denser salt water, but the
    two layers don't mix. This condition slows boat travel
    considerably. (see also slackwater)

delta: the mouth of the river, the area where the river widens and
    spreads out, separating into many different channels as it
    joins another body of water. A delta can be hard to navigate
    due to shifting channels and sandbars.

eddy: a rough current in the water, running in circles like a whirl-
    pool, or opposite to the main current

floodplain: the area of fairly flat land in a river valley, stretching
    from the banks of the river to the edges of the valley. Both
    the Arkansas River and the Mississippi River have broad
    floodplains, prone to disastrous flooding.

gandydancer: a railroad worker, especially those laying the tracks,
    possibly in reference to the Gandy Shovel Company, though
    the existence of such a company has not been substantiated.

gunwales: the top edges of the sides of the boat

levee: a dike or embankment that helps regulate water levels in the
    areas alongside a river or other body of water. Levees can be
    natural or manmade.

meander: (noun) a river bend (definition by Terri Whetstone Hansen)

oxbow lake: a crescent or U-shaped lake formed when a river bend or meander is cut off from the main river

riprap: large rocks along the shore to help prevent erosion

sawyer: a fallen tree stuck on the bottom of river which is a bugger to canoe around or over. (definition by Kris Troska.)

slackwater: an area of water in a river without current, often protected by a sandbar or bay; water that is motionless or still. (see also dead water)

snag: a branch, stump, or log stuck in the riverbottom and rising to the top or near the top of the water, likely to pierce a boat

strainers: overhanging branches that lean into the water and catch debris and canoers, while allowing the water to pass on through. Strainers are dangerous because the force of the water can trap the unlucky person against the obstruction.

sweep: much like a strainer, a sweep is a tree that has fallen so that the branches drag the water.

through-truss bridge: a bridge supported by a framework of connecting metal beams bracing above, below and along the sides of the bridge deck, allowing traffic to travel throug the framework from one end to the other.

turnbuckle: hardware with threaded screws on both ends, used to tighten lines without twisting them.

Photo Credits

Cover photo: front Terri Karsten /2012

Cover photo: back: AS/ 1949

pg 3 Brian Evert/2012/ PG

pg 4 map by Kayla Fayerweather

pg 6 AS/ 1949

pg 7 AS/ 1949

pg 8 AS/ 1949

pg 9 AS/ 1949

pg 13 ©Terri Karsten/ 2012

pg 14 origin unknown/1949/ PD

pg 16 AS/ 1949

pg 17 AS/ 1949

pg 18 AS 1949

pg 19 map by Kayla Fayerweather

pg 20 all 4 photos: AS/ 1949

pg 21 both photos: Steve Eller /Historic American Engineering Record/ Library of Congress/ 1968/ PD

pg 22 Clayton Fraser/ US Dept. of Interior/ NPS, 1984/ PD

pg 25 US Army Corps of Engineers/ circa 1979/ PD

pg 28 AS, 1949

pg 29 map by Kayla Fayerweather

pg 32 Billy Hathorn/ 2010/ CC-BY-SA 3.0 (//creativecommons.org/licenses/by-sa/3.0/deed.en)

pg 33 AS 1949

pg 38 *Hutchinson News-Herald*/ June 28, 1949/copyright not renewed/PD

pg 39 anonymous postcard circa 1949/ PD

pg 41 top: ©AP WirePhoto, PG
bottom: ©*Wichita Eagle,* June 1949/ PG

pg 47 ©*The Arkansas City Traveler*, July 1, 1949/PG

pg 48 AS/ 1949

pg 49 map by Kayla Fayerweather

pg 51 ©*Ponca City News*/ July 6, 1949/ PG

pg 56 ©Beryl Ford Collection/ Rotary Club of Tulsa, Tulsa City-County Library and Tulsa Historical Society/1917/CC-BY-SA 3.0 (//commons.wikimedia.org/wiki/File:11thStreetBridge1917.jpg)

pg 57 AS/ 1949

pg 62 AS/ 1949

pg 63 Both photos: AS/1949

pg 64 AS/ 1949

pg 65 map by Kayla Fayerweather

pg 68 Doug Wertman (http://flickr.com/photos/12227796@N08)/2009/CC-BY-SA 2.0 (//creativecommons.org/licenses/by/2.0/deed.en)

pg 69 AS/ 1949
pg 72 AS/ 1949
pg 74 ©Photolitherland at en.wikipedia (http://en.wikipedia.org)(talk)Chris Litherland /2009/ CC-BY-SA 3.0(//creativecommons.org/licenses/by-sa/3.0/deed.en)
pg 76 BartLIV/2007/PD
pg 79 Both photos: Johnnie Gray/ ©*Arkansas Gazette,* July 24, 1949/ PG
pg 80 Brian Evert/2012/PG
pg 83 AS/ 1949
pg 85 Dick Henke, 1949
pg 88 AS/ 1949
pg 89 map by Kayla Fayerweather
pg 90 ©John Weeks/2008/CC-BY-SA 3.0 (//creativecommons.org/licenses/by-sa/3.0/deed.en)
pg 91 Department of Defense/1938/ PD
pg 94 ©Heironymous Rowe/2010/ CC-BY-SA 3.0 (//creativecommons.org/licenses/by-sa/3.0/deed.en)
pg 105 ©Richard Rutter (http://www.flick.com/people/ 27616775AN00) /2005/ CC-BY-SA 2.0 (//creativecommons.org/licenses/by-sa/2.0/deed.en)
pg 107 Both photos: AS/ 1949

pg 111 ©*Times Picayune*/August 12, 1949/ PG
pg 114 AS/1949
pg 115 AS/1949
pg 116 Louisiana News Company, LA/1930-1950/ PD
pg 123 ©*The Denver Post*/August 21, 1949/PG
pg 124 AS, 1949

Acknowledgments

This book would not have been possible without the generous help of a great many people. I wish to thank all of them, with particular thanks to the following:

- Alyssa Koenig for transcribing the entire diary and Dick's letters, as well as many other editorial tasks,
- Cindy Sarmento, Cheri Kretsch, and Wayne Henke for their enthusiastic support and cooperation,
- Kayla Fayerweather for reading my mind to produce maps I could only imagine,
- Kris Troska and Mark Meier for proofreading and editing,
- The research librarians at Winona Public Library, Winona, MN; Natchez Public Library, Natchez, MS; and Little Rock Public Library, Little Rock, Arkansas,
- The staff and volunteers at Pulaski County Historical Society, Pueblo County Historical Society, and The Arkansas Department of Parks and Tourism, and Yell County Historical Society, Arkansas,
- All the editors and assitant editors at the various newspapers for their assitance in locating articles and photos of the trip,
- The writer's groups in Onalaska and LaCrescent who listened to early versions and offered advice and support,
- My mother, the packrat, who saved all of John Evert's letters from the trip, along with numerous newspaper clippings,
- And of course: Johnny, Dick, and Jerry, who undertook this marvelous journey and told the stories to their children, thus whetting an insatiable search for our own adventures.

Index of places

www.ingramcontent.com/pod-product-compliance
Lightning Source LLC
Chambersburg PA
CBHW072025040426
42447CB00009B/1740